"I am pleased to recommend *The Crescent ┊* by Nabeel Jabbour. By stepping into the shoes of Muslims and looking through their eyes, Jabbour helps Christians understand them in these troubled days, love them as God does, and express their witness more relevantly."

—J. DUDLEY WOODBERRY, dean emeritus and senior professor of Islamic studies, Fuller Theological Seminary

"Unfortunately many Christians follow the confrontational approach with Muslims rather than an approach of compassion, understanding, and love. This is why when I read Nabeel Jabbour's book, I recovered a sense of confidence in myself as a Muslim who is a follower of Christ and began to get rid of my feelings of guilt for coming to Christ from such a "stigmatized" background. Indeed some of what I read, written by my western Christian brothers, contributed over the years to making me feel like a cultural convict, because they kept undermining the thing by which I culturally live—my worldview—which in no way takes away from my faith in Jesus Christ as my Lord and Savior."

—DR. NORDDINE AL ARABI, professor; author

"I am delighted to see this book get published. I wish every Christian in the West could read it, as it adds a dimension of grace to the debates currently being waged over Islam. I know of no other book like it."

—JIM PETERSEN, missionary; author

"I know of no better book that demonstrates the impact of an author's unique background and experiences. Equally important, I know of no book that more insightfully and penetratingly addresses the 'invisible' perversions of understanding that arise when Westerners try to understand the Arabs and the Muslims. Page after page will take your breath away!"

—DR. RALPH D. WINTER, chancellor, William Carey International University

"What Nabeel Jabbour has written is very important at a time when anti-Arab and anti-Musli sentiments run so high in Evangelical circles. What you read here will help you to see things in the Middle East as a Arab Christian does. It is likely to impact you in ways that are unexpected and necessary."

—TONY CAMPOLO, PhD, Easter University, St. Davids, PA

"This book offers vitally needed bridges of understanding and compassion between different worldviews, theologies, and historical experiences. As Dr. Jabbour states in his introductory remarks, this is a book intended to help Western Christian readers better comprehend Muslim perspectives and beliefs and thus dispel commonly held misunderstandings and dehumanizing stereotypes."

—DR. PHILIP ZIMBARDO, professor emeritus, Stanford University; author of *The Lucifer Effect: Understanding How Good People Turn Evil*; also known for his 1971 Stanford Mock Prison experiment

"One of the finest and most insightful books on the beliefs and cultural context of Islam. Every Christian seeking to understand the Muslim worldview and the relationship between East and West must read this book."

—ALI ELHAJJ, director, The Bethlehem Christmas Project

" 'Why do they hate us?' Nabeel Jabbour's timely book tells us why and what we can do about it."

—JAMES FOX, British film actor, *The Servant* ( '63), *Remains of the Day* ('93), and *Charlie and the Chocolate Factory* ('04)

"Awesome, excellent, well written, clear—what a gift! It is a must-read."

—CHUCK WENGER, Christian leader, Board Member - Middle East Peace Initiative

"This book has brought me the greatest insight and understanding I have ever had into the ways in which Muslims see us as Christians. It is challenging and disturbing in the way attitudes are exposed. It is a must-read."

—SANDRA WHEATLEY, England

"Nabeel Jabbour's important new book will open your eyes to the real world of Islam, not the one so often caricatured in the media. Deeply biblical with study and discussion questions, the book is based on a lifetime of dialogue and witness among Muslims. This book will warm your heart and fire your soul to reach the 'other' children of Abraham for Jesus."

—REVEREND STEPHEN SIZER, author

# DR. NABEEL T. JABBOUR

# THE
# CRESCENT
## THROUGH THE EYES OF
## THE CROSS

*Insights from an Arab Christian*

NAVPRESS

Discipleship Inside Out™

NavPress is the publishing ministry of The Navigators, an international Christian organization and leader in personal spiritual development. NavPress is committed to helping people grow spiritually and enjoy lives of meaning and hope through personal and group resources that are biblically rooted, culturally relevant, and highly practical.

**For a free catalog go to www.NavPress.com or call 1.800.366.7788 in the United States or 1.800.839.4769 in Canada.**

ISBN-13: 978-1-60006-195-0

Cover design by The DesignWorks Group, Charles Brock, www.thedesignworksgroup.com
Cover image by Shutterstock
Creative Team: Don Simpson, Kathy Mosier, Darla Hightower, Arvid Wallen, Kathy Guist

Some of the anecdotal illustrations in this book are true to life and are included with the permission of the persons involved. All other illustrations are composites of real situations, and any resemblance to people living or dead is coincidental.

Unless otherwise identified, all Scripture quotations in this publication are taken from the *HOLY BIBLE: NEW INTERNATIONAL VERSION®* (NIV®). Copyright © 1973, 1978, 1984 by International Bible Society. Used by permission of Zondervan Publishing House. All rights reserved. Other version used is *THE MESSAGE* (MSG). Copyright © 1993, 1994, 1995, 1996, 2000, 2001, 2002, 2005. Used by permission of NavPress Publishing Group. Also quoted is *The Noble Qur'an: The First American Translation and Commentary* by T. B. Irving. Copyright © 1992, Amana Books. All rights reserved.

Library of Congress Cataloging-in-Publication Data

Jabbur, Nabil.
   The Crescent through the eyes of the Cross : insights from an Arab Christian / Nabeel T. Jabbour. -- 1st ed.
      p. cm.
   Includes bibliographical references.
   ISBN 978-1-60006-195-0
   1. Apologetics. 2. Christianity and other religions--Islam. 3. Missions to Muslims. I. Title.
BT1170.J33 2008
261.2'7--dc22

                              2007035272

Printed in the United States of America

3 4 5 6 7 8 / 13 12 11 10

*To*

*our prayer partners,*
*who have journeyed with us over the years.*
*Your partnership is invaluable.*

# CONTENTS

PART THREE: THE RECEIVER — CONNECTING WITH MUSLIMS

# FOREWORD

During the years Nabeel and Barbara Jabbour lived in Cairo, Egypt, I visited them regularly. Their home was on the third floor in a three-story apartment building situated in a residential part of the city. A small guest room had been constructed on the roof of the building, a stair climb up from the Jabbour apartment. That is where I would stay. It was a perfect place, very comfortable except for one thing. Every morning at the crack of dawn, I would hear an electronic click just outside my door. There would be a bit of static, and over a microphone I would hear someone clearing his throat. Then the call would begin with *"Allah-u Akbar"*: "God is great/transcendent." The words would blare through the speaker system of the mosque that stood a few meters away. The initial click would be enough to wake me up, and moments later I would be wide awake, feeling frustrated by this untimely invasion into my night of rest. As the call droned on, I would lie there concocting futile plots to disable the speaker system.

At breakfast time I would descend the stairs that led to the kitchen, still nursing my frustration and expecting some commiserating from

Nabeel and Barbara, since their bedroom was just one floor below mine. But it never came up. Finally, after several days into my first visit, I asked them how they managed to cope with this daily intrusion. Nabeel replied that at first he, too, had found it disruptive, but when he began to treat it as *his* call to prayer, it ceased to be a problem. He would awaken with the call and spend the first minutes of the day in prayer. It was as simple as that.

This spirit characterizes the Jabbours. Over the years, in Cairo and in other parts of Egypt, I watched them relate to Reformed Protestants, Coptic Christians, and Muslims, all with an apparent ease that belied the true difficulty of such a challenge. They embodied the first rule of successful cross-cultural communication of the gospel. The apostle Paul summarized the rule with these words:

> I have voluntarily become a servant to any and all in order to reach a wide range of people: religious, nonreligious, meticulous moralists, loose-living immoralists . . . whoever. I didn't take on their way of life. I kept my bearings in Christ—but I entered their world and tried to experience things from their point of view. I've become just about every sort of servant there is in my attempts to lead those I meet into a God-saved life. (1 Corinthians 9:19-22, MSG)

To state the rule in a nutshell, *the messenger adapts to the people he is seeking to win.*

This is not easy. To accomplish this, one must first confront the giant of one's own ethnocentrism, that natural tendency to consider one's own ideas and ways as being the right and only—or at least the best—approach. To get past this to the point where one can empathize with the feelings and fears of someone of another culture is no small feat. It is, in fact, so difficult that most people don't even want to think about it. But think about it we must. Today, followers of Christ all over the world are being faced with the challenge to understand and relate to a people we have, historically, pretty much ignored: the Muslims.

In the last decade Islam has grabbed the world's attention. The world as we have known it is changing as opinions and loyalties polarize around Western and Islamic cultures. Islam itself is in the throes of change as different factions within it struggle for supremacy—or survival.

But these struggles are secondary to the one that is going on for the minds and souls of individual Muslims. Our tendency is to lump the structures of Islam and the individuals within those structures into a single caricature—and thereby feed our prejudices. But whatever you might think of Islam as a religion and a culture should have little bearing on how you relate to a person who is Muslim. Our calling as followers of Christ is to love our neighbors because God loves them, even if we might perceive some of them as our enemies.

Love is a verb, a call to action. It calls us not only to seek to understand these neighbors but also to serve them in ways that reflect God's love. How else will they ever *see* the kingdom of God?

How, you wonder, could this actually happen? Where would one even begin? This book is an excellent starting point. It offers the reader a unique opportunity to engage in the story of Muslims and to sense what they think and feel. It will help you take those essential first steps toward adapting to people we seek to win.

JIM PETERSEN

# ACKNOWLEDGMENTS

I am deeply grateful for the insights and contributions that a variety of friends have made to this book. I could not have written it without their help. The hours and the effort they have spent reviewing the manuscript are invaluable. *You know who you are.* I am also grateful to the staff of NavPress for making this book a reality.

# PREFACE

On a trip to Santa Fe, New Mexico, in 2004, I was struck by one of the most stunning sculptures I have ever seen. This piece of art had two interrelated scenes back to back, separated by a door. On one side was a Native American man in a fierce snowstorm, knocking at the door of a log cabin and pleading for refuge and warmth. On the other side of the door was a warm room with a terrified mother holding a shotgun while the woman's frightened three-year-old daughter clung to her dress. The terrified mother was refusing to open the door.

Fear of the unknown. We tend to fear what we do not understand. There are things we definitely need to fear, but we need to differentiate between healthy and unhealthy fears.

Recently, as I was planning for a trip from Colorado Springs to Chicago, I was wondering what book to take with me to read on the airplane. Two books came to mind. One was written in English by A'la al-Maududi, who was a radical Pakistani Muslim. Al-Maududi and the famous Sayyid Qutb were two main theologians of Islamic fundamentalism in the twentieth century. The other book was written in Arabic by an Egyptian pastor about the history of Christianity in the Middle East before the advent of Islam. As I considered these two books, I thought it might be safer to take the book written in English rather than the one written in Arabic. Would those sitting next to me feel safer if they saw me reading a book in English, although it was written by al-Maududi, rather than a Christian book in Arabic? People tend to fear what they do not understand.

The purpose of this book is to help readers understand and develop compassion for Muslims. Understanding and love help dispel a great deal of our unhealthy fears. We need to go beyond mere tolerance of the Muslims in our midst. Tolerance can still keep the Muslims at arm's length: "You live your life, and I'll live mine." Western Christians need to learn to consciously live with Muslims and understand their worldview. Some of us have Muslim workmates, others have Muslim neighbors, and others see Muslims when we go shopping. There are still others of us, though, who do not see any Muslims in our towns or cities. And yet every one of us gets reminded, almost on a daily basis, of the fact that Muslims are here to stay as we see them on the television screens in our living rooms. Some of us take them even to our bedrooms as we have some sleepless moments struggling with anxiety, hatred, and prejudice against them. Whether we like it or not, we share our globe with them. Sooner better than later, every one of us needs to learn to live with Muslims and understand their worldview. Understanding how they think—and *why* they think the way they do—is absolutely essential. Understanding triggers compassion and makes acceptance possible. Consider the story Brennan Manning included in his book *Abba's Child*:

> Author Stephen Covey recalled an incident while riding the New York City subway one Sunday morning. The few passengers aboard were reading the newspaper or dozing. . . . Covey

was engrossed in reading when a man accompanied by several small children boarded at the next stop. In less than a minute, bedlam erupted. The kids ran up and down the aisle shouting, screaming, and wrestling with one another on the floor. Their father made no attempt to intervene.

The elderly passengers shifted nervously. Stress became distress. Covey waited patiently. Surely the father would do something to restore order. . . . Frustration mounted. After an unduly generous pause, Covey turned to the father and said kindly, "Sir, perhaps you could restore order here by telling your children to come back and sit down." "I know I should do something," the man replied. "We just came from the hospital. Their mother died an hour ago. I just don't know what to do."[1]

Although I am a Christian writing to Christians, the focal point of this book is the fictional story line about an Egyptian Muslim, an international student in the United States with the name Ahmad. I know Ahmad well because I have met him in hundreds of Muslims over the past five decades. This character, beginning in chapter 2, will describe concisely fifteen aspects of the Muslim worldview. Chapter 3 will include a short presentation of the views of Ahmad's father, who lives in Egypt. Chapter 4 is written by Ahmad's sister. Both chapters 3 and 4 will shed more light on the issues raised by Ahmad in chapter 2.

Ahmad, his father, and his sister represent both *fiction* and *reality*. Ahmad is a composite of Muslims I have known, international students and people in the Middle East. I have known these Muslims either personally or through their writings. Ahmad's ideas, and those of his father and sister, are actual representations of the Muslim worldview; this is *reality*. The people I have imagined here and called Ahmad and Fatima, as well as how my relationship with Ahmad developed, are *fiction*.

In this book, I would like to remind you of "your neighbor" the Muslim. Muslims live on the same planet with you, although they might look strange and seem hard to understand. I would like to invite you to have a cross-cultural experience of seeing them through God's eyes and stretching your tolerance zone to look at the world through their eyes. I am inviting you to put on Jesus and the cross as you look at—and embrace—the crescent in order to develop compassion and understanding. Are you ready for this adventure?

Chapters 1 through 4 are important scene-setting chapters to help us understand the Muslim mind. Beginning with chapter 1, each chapter will close with thought-provoking questions for reflection and discussion.

For those readers who are interested in going deeper into some of the issues that Ahmad raises, I will make available an *addendum* that looks more closely at *current events as they are perceived by Muslims*. This additional material will cover the Crusades, colonialism, Israel's modern history, eschatology, and the danger we face of a holy world war between Christendom and Islam. The addendum will be available as an e-mail attachment *only to those who have read the book* and request it. To obtain a copy, please write me at nabeel@nabeeljabbour.com.

In the pages ahead, Ahmad, in his composite presentation, will address fifteen issues under three categories: Your (Christian) Message; You, the (Christian) Messenger; and Me, the (Muslim) Receiver. The major portion of this book will unpack and address the issues of the "Your Message" and "Me, the Receiver" sections, also touching on the "You, the Messenger" section. In the addendum, I will explore further the issues of the "You, the Messenger" section by taking the reader into summaries of some very helpful books on several controversial topics.

PART ONE

# SETTING THE STAGE

MEET AHMAD

# CHAPTER 1

# WHY BOTHER?

Years ago I was introduced to a Muslim in Colorado Springs who was unemployed and an alcoholic. I did not know immediately about his alcoholism. I tried to help this man get a job working for a friend of my family's. Very soon after he got the job, I discovered that he started giving our friend a hard time. Then he got fired.

A few days later, my wife and I found out that this person had called our telephone company and, with their permission, had used our phone number to make international calls as if it were a calling card. When the phone company finally called us to investigate, we were shocked that the company had given him permission to use our account. Their reasoning was that we were good customers and had a good record. They also said that this Muslim knew the name of our older son, as if the name of our son were a password.

This man's abuse of my trust made me furious. Very quickly my relationship with him terminated, and I did not want anything more to do with him. I wanted to get him out of my hair, and if he ended up in prison, he deserved it. Why bother with him?

Twelve years later in 2004, I came to know a computer expert in Colorado Springs who was an American evangelical Christian. He was the best computer expert I had ever known, and in some ways, he became a friend. In 2005, he bought a computer business. He asked me if he could borrow some money for one year, and in return he would pay me interest and would fix my computer free during that year whenever repair was needed.

My wife and I decided to help this man succeed in his new business, so we loaned him $1,000 and told him we did not want any interest. He asked me if I could help him by getting some of my friends to loan him money as well, but I did not feel free to do that. A few months into the year, his business was not picking up and he disappeared completely from our city. He did not answer phone calls or e-mails, and the address on the receipt that he gave us for the $1,000 turned out to be fake. He sold his office space to a new company, and nobody knew where he was.

Again, I got furious for a brief time. My wife convinced me that we should *release* the $1,000 and not try to find the man or see a lawyer. Now, as I think of him, I am amazed that I am completely free of any resentment or bitterness. I wish I could communicate to him that he is completely forgiven. I do hope that one day he will return to the Lord and that his relationship with God will be restored.

Why was my reaction to the computer expert different from my reaction to the Muslim? I think I handled the second situation better because I had grown spiritually since the first situation occurred and because financially we were better off. Now as I think of it, I wish my reaction to the Muslim man had been with grace rather than with anger.

## IT IS EASY TO BE PREJUDICED

Many people in the West have arrived at the conclusion, openly or discretely, that there is a clash of civilizations, "ours" and "theirs." "A line has been drawn in the sand. We are on one side and the Muslims are on the other," one famous American televangelist declared. We Christians who live in non-Muslim countries are bombarded with the message that "we," the Christians, are the rational, the educated, the sophisticated, and the civilized, while "they," the Muslims, are the strange people with the strange accents and strange dress who adhere to a strange religion that breeds terrorism, hatred, and backwardness.

Islam, as a religion, and Muslims, as people, are indeed strange phenomena to Christians around the world. As I have said earlier, "It is relatively easy for us to judge their dedication as extremism, their willingness to lay down their lives for the service of God as terrorism, and their holistic view of life as fanaticism. Furthermore, it is easy for us to judge their passion for justice as revenge, their convictions as dogmatism, and their sense of dignity and honor as empty pride."[1]

This is not a new trend. Edward Said, in his book *Orientalism*, described a stage (the Orient) on which a drama is put together by a dramatist (the Western Christian):

> In the depths of this oriental stage stands a prodigious cultural repertoire whose individual items evoke a fabulously rich world: the Sphinx, Cleopatra, Eden, Sodom and Gomorrah, Isis and Osiris, Sheba, Babylon, the Genii, the Magi, Nineveh, Mohamet, and dozens more settings, in some cases names only, half imagined, half known, monsters, devils, heroes, terrors, pleasures, desires.[2]

Muhammad, the prophet of Islam, does not escape the judgment of the Western analyst and critic either. Dante puts him in Canto 28 of the *Inferno*.

There are about 1.4 billion Muslims in the world. They constitute more than 20 percent of the world's population. It is predicted that by the year 2020 they will become a quarter of humanity, and the percentage will consistently go up. Americans have felt protected by large oceans and distance, but 9/11 and the events that followed smashed that sense of security and safety. The war in Iraq, its aftermath, and the mass media coverage of it have reinforced in the minds of many Christians around the world the currently popular idea of a "clash of civilizations" in action.[3] Before we delve into the details of the oncoming clash of cultures, let me tell you a little about myself.

## MY BACKGROUND

I am an Arab and a fourth-generation born-again Christian. I was born in Syria, grew up in Lebanon, and, along with my wife and sons, lived in Egypt from 1975 to 1990 as a missionary with The Navigators. As far as I know, my family goes back to first-century Christianity and to Acts chapter 2. My great-grandfather had an encounter with Christ as a result of prolonged reading of a copy of the New Testament given to him by American missionary and educator Daniel Bliss.*

In all three countries of the Middle East where I lived — Syria, Lebanon, and Egypt — I coexisted with Muslims. There were no oceans that separated me from them. I went to school with them, I played sports with them, and I always thought I understood them and appreciated their worldview. But a huge change came for me during our

---

* Daniel Bliss was the founder of the American University in Beirut, Lebanon, which used to be called the Syrian Protestant College.

years in Egypt. The ministry we had with Muslims in Egypt allowed me to see another face of Islam and Muslims.

From 1987 to 1990, I participated in a doctorate program by correspondence. I was living in Cairo, the best place in the world for my field of study. Cairo is the intellectual capital of Islam, and my study focused on Islam in general and on Islamic fundamentalism in particular. During those three years, most of what I read was written by Muslims in Arabic. As I immersed myself in Islam, I learned to look at it as a phenomenon rather than projecting my prejudice onto it and arriving too early at conclusions. In short, I learned to stand in the shoes of Muslims and to see Islam through their eyes.

## CULTURE SHOCK

We moved to Colorado Springs in January 1991 in the midst of the first Gulf War. It was quite a transition for us to move from Egypt to America during a war. Very soon I started teaching an adult Sunday school class on Islam to about seventy American evangelicals. The class lasted for more than six months. During the last session, I wanted to bring the class to a close by using a practical application. I drew three columns on the large whiteboard.

On top of the first column I wrote, "How do Muslims in Iraq evaluate the Gulf War?" On top of the second column I wrote, "How do redneck* Americans evaluate the Gulf War?" (My use of *redneck* was not meant to demean any group but simply to apply a popular shorthand to mean those secular folk who are socially and politically hyperconservative.) On top of the third column I wrote, "How should American Christians evaluate the Gulf War?" It took some time for us

---

\* A popular expression defined by Webster as a white member of the Southern rural laboring class in the United States.

to fill up the first column. The second column filled up quickly and was very long. When we came to the third column, it was a challenge to most of the people there. I reminded them that they were neither Iraqi Muslims nor redneck Americans.

Further, I reminded them that they were Christians who were Americans. Their primary loyalty is not to America but to the expansion of the gospel among the nations to advance the kingdom of God. At the end of the class, one of the men came to me and told me that was the most difficult Sunday school class he had ever attended. He told me he was tempted to walk out of class. I asked him why he didn't walk out, and his response was, "I kept reminding myself that I am not a redneck American. I am a Christian who is an American."

## AHMAD, MY NEW FRIEND

Since we moved to the States, I had the opportunity to become acquainted with Muslim international students who came to the U.S. and Canada for graduate studies. These international students were mostly from the Arab world, some from Iran and other Muslim countries. Furthermore, the years I spent in the Middle East provided me with ample opportunities to come to know many Muslims personally and still others through their writings. I must admit, a few Muslims have become some of my heroes.

Rabi'a al-'Adawiyya, who was an eighth-century mystic woman in Iraq, is one of my heroes. As a child, she was a slave. Over the years, she demonstrated a deep love for God to the degree that her owner set her free. Because of her fame as a woman of God, many Muslim women came to her and asked her to mentor them. With time, she started something like a convent for Muslim women. Here is one of her famous prayers that I will paraphrase into our terminology: "Lord, why do I love you? Do I love you out of fear of going to hell? If this is my motive then send me to hell. Or do I love you out of a motive of wanting to go to paradise? If this is my motive, then deprive me of paradise. O God, please purify my motives. Help me to love you for your own sake. Because you are worthy of all my love and all my worship."

I wish you could meet all my Muslim friends. In this book, I will attempt to convey to you *how they feel and what they think*. Since it is impossible for you to meet all of them, I have invented Ahmad. As I mentioned earlier, he is *not one person* but a *composite of many Muslims I know*. But he is *very real*, and the things he has to say will help us understand how Muslims feel about us. *So our story begins.*

In the early summer of 2006, I was preaching at the Sunday services of one of the churches in Colorado Springs. I spoke on the topic "Making Sense of 9/11," and in my message I shared my passion for Muslims. After the service, a man who looked Arab came to talk to me and expressed his gratitude for the way I demonstrated respect for Muslims. From his accent, I could tell right away that he was an Arab. His name was Ahmad Abdul Mun'im. I was surprised to meet a Muslim in a church. Very quickly I found out that he was an Egyptian, and we started conversing in Arabic. He was in Colorado Springs for the next few months, so I agreed to get together with him soon. Over those months we spent a great deal of time together, and he became a very good friend.

I learned quite a bit about Ahmad, including the fact that he had come to the States one month before 9/11 to study for a PhD program. In Cairo he had attended the American University of Cairo, where he earned his master's degree. He came from a relatively small Muslim family—father, mother, and a sister—but his extended family was huge. His father, a physician, instilled in him the value of education and hard work, and his family was willing to sacrifice a great deal to provide for him the best education possible.

Ahmad told me that the first week after arriving in the States some

Muslim students at the university tried to recruit him to the Muslim association, but he refused to live in a Muslim bubble while in America. It had been his dream for years to come to the States and do his graduate studies. It was obvious to me from our first get-together that he had deep roots in his Muslim faith. He did not come to America to party as some Muslims do. He was very focused on getting his doctoral degree but at the same time wanted to have a cross-cultural experience. Before coming to the States he had never seen American football, cheerleaders, ice hockey, and baseball. His favorite sport was soccer, which he had always called football until he came to America. His favorite football team in Egypt was the same one that my family had supported during our time there. Talking about soccer contributed to strengthening my connection with him.

In his desire to have a cross-cultural experience in America, he was like a child with excitement, innocence, and eagerness for the great adventure. This excitement was dampened a great deal, however, by the events of 9/11 that took place shortly after his arrival. As he talked about his memories of 9/11, it was a very painful time for both of us. He recalled how he was glued to the TV for days and how he watched the events with deep pain and frustration. For days he was stunned and very angry with the fanatical Muslims. At the same time, he wished that Americans would not use a broad brush and consider all Muslims terrorists or suspects. He also wished that Americans would move beyond the horrific events and try to understand why the gap is so wide between Arabs and the West.

Ahmad started noticing that many people related to him with caution once they heard his thick Arab accent and found out that he was a Muslim. The politically correct smiles toward him hid suspicion, fear, and a desire not to connect with him. There came a time when he hated leaving his apartment and going to the university or the supermarket. At that critical time, he told me that it would have been very easy for him to connect with the Muslims on campus by joining the Muslim association, and thereby end up in a Muslim bubble, but with great determination he resisted that temptation.

He wanted very much for people to know that not all Muslims are terrorists and that neither he nor anyone in his extended family was a fundamentalist or even a sympathizer with the fundamentalists. Not many people gave him a chance. Many were suspicious, fearful, or insecure when they talked with him. He told me that at times he felt like he came from a different planet. On the verge of tears, he told me how one of the students at the university who was an evangelical Christian came and asked him bluntly to prove to him that he was not a "sleeper," or a terrorist in disguise.

What I liked very much about Ahmad, though, was his open mind in addition to being a practicing and committed Muslim. His deep roots in his faith and in the Egyptian culture did not make him prejudiced against people from other religions and other cultures. He found that the friendliest Americans, especially after 9/11, were some American evangelicals. Some other evangelicals were very judgmental, and he avoided them. He invited some of the friendly evangelicals to his apartment and cooked Egyptian food for them. Some of them invited him to their homes and to their churches. By the time he visited the church where I was preaching, he told me that he had already visited about ten churches.

What surprised me even more was that Ahmad started reading the Bible in addition to his regular reading of the Qur'an. His favorite section in the Bible was the Gospels, especially Matthew 5–7, the Sermon on the Mount. I was amazed at how much he had read even from the Old Testament. He had many questions about Christianity in America and was worried about the growing gap between Christians and Muslims. He shared with me his embarrassment about how some Muslims reacted with violence to the Danish cartoons. In the same breath he told me that he was shocked by the declarations of some famous Christian leaders who spoke against Islam and against his prophet Muhammad.

God gave me grace in Ahmad's eyes. We connected very deeply. Having lived in Egypt with my family for fifteen years and having studied Islam made it easy for me to befriend Ahmad. During those summer months, we had many long visits together. The last time was the most significant. He helped me see the world through his eyes as I listened to him not only with my ears but also with my heart. As a result of what he shared with me, *I will never look at the world the same way again.*

The worldview that he shared with me is what we will explore in the next chapter.

## QUESTIONS FOR REFLECTION AND DISCUSSION

1. Some people assume that there is a clash of civilizations taking place between the Muslim world and the West. Others think the clash is between fundamentalists in all religions. What do you think?

2. How would "redneck Americans" evaluate the "war against terror"? How would Muslims around the world evaluate America's "war on terror"? How should Christians (God's ambassadors) evaluate America's "war on terror"?

CHAPTER 2

# AHMAD'S WORLDVIEW

I found Ahmad, my new friend, to be very loyal to and proud of his family, his country, and his religion. He was so open-minded that at times I wished I were as open-minded as he was. One of the verses from the Qur'an that he frequently repeated had to do with the fact that "there should be no compulsion in religion" (Surah 2:256). He assured me that he did not want to try to convert me to Islam, and, in humility and with politeness, he asked me not to try to convert him to Christianity. He was worried that if we tried to convert one another we might end up severing our relationship. He wanted very much, though, to talk about Christ and about the issues in the Bible that he did not understand. Our times together in Colorado Springs, and since then by e-mail, have become very precious memories in a very special friendship.

Ahmad told me that he had become very familiar with the methods Christians use in talking about Christ and in trying to convert other people to Christianity. Sometimes they all sound the same, as if the Christians have memorized the same verses from the Bible and have all been trained to propagate their religion by the same mentor. He told me that he had been exposed to the "Four Spiritual Laws," the Bridge to Life illustration, and "Steps to Peace with God."

He shared with me his frustration in not knowing how to explain to those zealous Christian friends that he has a different worldview. He tried to help them by standing in their shoes and explaining to them that there are things in *their message* that do not make sense to Muslims. At other times he tried to stand in the shoes of fellow Muslims in Egypt and around the world and then explain to his Christian friends why Muslims are *frustrated by Christianity and by the West*. Furthermore, he shared with me how evangelical friends have no idea why *he is not willing to leave Islam and become a Christian*.

I listened to him and expressed my longings to understand his worldview. I promised that I would listen to him with a deep desire to understand. One time he looked me straight in the eyes and asked, "Are you willing to listen even though I might end up stepping on your toes?" I assured him that I would listen attentively because I want to learn to see the world through his eyes. So he shared with me that after months of trying to communicate with his Christian friends in bits and pieces, he decided to write down a description of his worldview. He had been waiting for an opportunity when some Christians in a church or a home setting would ask him to describe his worldview. So he had it all prepared, and I provided him with the first opportunity. He asked me if he could bring his computer memory stick with him next time so that he could print it on my printer.

He was eager to read to a Christian a text into which he had poured his soul. Yet at the same time he was anxious that he might offend me and lose my friendship. I assured him again that I would truly listen because I wanted to learn. I even asked him if he would allow me to save it on my computer and use it in my own speaking and writing. He gave me permission to do so.

## OUR LAST SESSION TOGETHER

One day before our last session, I had mixed feelings. I wished that Ahmad would live in the same city as me permanently. I wished his visit to Colorado Springs were longer. Yet at the same time I was grateful to God that my relationship with him would continue through e-mail and phone calls. I anxiously desired to defend or correct some misconceptions on his part, yet I promised God that I would be willing to listen to him with an open mind. I pleaded to God that somehow Ahmad would see Jesus in my attitude of respect, humility, and willingness to listen and learn.

Ahmad arrived at our home for that final visit. My wife offered him some Lebanese sweets that he loved and his favorite drink, hot tea. I asked him if he had brought with him the computer memory stick, and he had. So we printed his presentation and then sat down in our living room. There was an atmosphere of sorrow because this was his last visit. The next day he would be flying back to his university town to continue his work on his PhD.

Ahmad broke the silence as he tried to express how much he was going to miss our times together. He asked me one more time if I was still willing to learn about his worldview. My answer was, "Absolutely!" So with his thick accent he started to read to me in English what he had written in the hope that one day he would have the opportunity to read it to interested Christians. Ahmad began:

*Bismilaah Rahman Rahim.* [In the name of God the Merciful the Compassionate.]

My name is Ahmad Abdul Mun'im. I have been here in the States since August 2001, one month before 9/11. I plan to go back home to Egypt when I finish my PhD program. During my stay here I was exposed to what you call evangelical Christians who invited me to their churches and tried to convert me to Christianity. My reaction to the Christianity that I was exposed to is the typical response of most Muslims around the world. At the same time it represents more specifically the *Arab* Muslim response.

One of those who tried to convert me asked me to explain to him why it is so difficult for me to convert and get integrated into Christianity. My response to him was, "There are three major reasons: *Your message; you, the messenger;* and *me, the receiver.*" Ladies and gentlemen, allow me to share with you what I shared with that friend.

I complimented Ahmad on the good introduction and shared with him how I liked his three categories: "Your Message"; "You, the Messenger"; and "Me, the Receiver."

## YOUR MESSAGE

1. Your Christian message appears to me as a foreign message. It is foreign in its vocabulary and foreign in its contents. Your religious vocabulary is so different from mine. I found this especially true when I was given an Arabic Bible to read. Although this Bible was written in Arabic, and my mother tongue is the Arabic language, I had a hard time understanding it. You Christians seem to have your own distinct religious language. Even the central figure in your religion, Jesus, has two names in this Arabic Bible. The Arab Christians call Jesus *Yasou'*, while we Muslims call Him *Isa*. Since you are so eager for us to understand your religion, why don't you use a language we can understand?

With pain in my heart I agreed with him on the fact that we Christians expect the Muslims to learn our Christian vocabulary in order to understand the message.

2. You see things and explain them with legal terminology, as if we are in a court. You talk so much about guilt and righteousness, sin and its penalty, condemnation and justification. I have been shown the "Four Spiritual Laws," the Bridge to Life illustration, and "Steps to Peace with God." They all follow logical syllogism and use legal terminology. My paradigm or lens through which I look at reality is not primarily that of guilt and righteousness like yours, but that of shame and honor, clean and unclean, fear and power. When I talk with you it feels like you are laying a guilt trip on me. Does your message have anything to say to me about my shame, my defilement, and my fear?

I was impressed by Ahmad's deep insight. Again I felt sad that we, as Christians, are failing these people in how we communicate the gospel. I thought of Jesus and how He spoke about the kingdom. He did not present the good news to the Eastern mind by using a strict, logical syllogism and putting the facts in this order:

1. God is holy.
2. Man is sinful.
3. There is a penalty for sin.
4. I (Christ) will pay the penalty.
5. You must believe in Me (Christ).

Jesus did not use this kind of syllogism; He taught in parables and used other paradigms.

3. When you do what you call "witnessing" to us, you assume that you understand our religion. You start with wrong assumptions by compar- ing our prophet Muhammad to Christ and comparing the Qur'an to the Bible. You think that you have figured us out and understand our theology. I am sorry to say you have a skewed understanding of our religion. A true

understanding of Islam necessitates that you compare Christ, the way you understand Him, to the Qur'an, the way we understand it. You believe that Christ is the eternal, uncreated Word of God, and we believe that the Qur'an, and not Muhammad, is the eternal, uncreated Word of God. The way you think of Christ is the way we think of the Qur'an. So who is equally as important in your religion as the prophet Muhammad is in ours? And what would your Bible compare to in our religion? Unless you solve this riddle, you will never understand our theology.

So many articles I have read since 9/11 make wrong comparisons. I agreed with him. Many Christians have a skewed understanding of Islam.

4. You seem to be very proud of your Bible. Please allow me to say something that will be very hard for you to hear. I believe that my book, the Qur'an, is more reliable than the Bible since it was dictated word by word through an angel sent by God. What you Christians believe about the Ten Commandments I believe about the whole of the Qur'an. The Qur'an was not written by men. It was dictated by God through an angel. Why should I leave my superior message and replace it with an inferior message that relies on a less reliable book?

With this one Ahmad really stepped on my toes, and he knew it. He looked at me after reading this point with a feeling of sorrow that he had hurt me. Yet he wanted to be honest with me. I felt sad too because I know that if Ahmad, my new friend, is willing to be fully honest with himself, he has to face the issue of the problems associated with mechanical inspiration. Are there mistakes in the Qur'an? Whose mistakes are they?

# YOU, THE MESSENGER

Ahmad continued,

Christianity is a Western religion, and we Muslims have a long history with you Christians. Let me share with you a bit of this history.

*Christianity is not a Western religion, I observed to myself. It is sad, though, that it has become a Western religion. I let Ahmad continue:*

5. The Crusades took place in the twelfth and thirteenth centuries. Wave after wave of armies kept coming to invade our lands for two hundred years. Western Christian countries sent their armies to Jerusalem to force upon Muslims a Christian *jihad* or "holy war" to clean up Jerusalem. Jerusalem is a city that is very special, not only to you, but to us, too. Sir Steven Runciman, your famous historian of the Crusades, said, "It was this blood-thirsty Christian fanaticism . . . that recreated the fanaticism of Islam." In your current U.S. Middle East policy, are you fueling and strengthening fanaticism within Islam? *In your neo-Crusader attitude, have you unleashed Islamic fanaticism and escalated violence?* In your desire to impose U.S.-style democracy on the Middle East, have you opened up a can of worms of Islamic fundamentalism?

*Wow! I was very impressed by how well-read he was. At the same time I was intrigued by how he connected the U.S. Middle East policy with the resurgence of Islamic fundamentalism.*

6. Every Muslim country in the world, except Iran, Turkey, Saudi Arabia, and Yemen, has been colonized by Western Christian nations such as Portugal, Britain, France, and Holland. These Western Christian countries came and depleted our natural resources. Under the guise of wanting

to civilize us and introduce democracy, they wished to impose upon us Muslims an inferior status. Some of our Muslim leaders wonder, *Is this same colonialism continuing today under a different name?* If the war in Iraq and its aftermath go your way, what kind of control will you exercise over Iraq and its neighbors?

As I listened to him addressing the issue of colonialism, I remembered reading the biography of Hasan al-Banna, the founder of the influential and revivalist Muslim Brotherhood in Egypt, and what he wrote about colonialism. I wondered if Ahmad, my friend, was partly influenced by al-Banna.

7. In 1948, Westerners planted Israel in the midst of us Arabs and the Muslim world. Prior to 1948, you did not want the Jews to leave Eastern Europe and Russia and come to America and England, so you planted them in Palestine. Since the creation of Israel in 1948, and the events that led to it, Israel has been a thorn in our side. Before that time Muslims did not have a big problem with Jews. Those responsible for the Spanish Inquisition and the Holocaust came from a Christian background, not a Muslim background!

Yes, Israel is a thorn in our side. This is not the feeling of Arab Muslims only but of all Muslims, my brothers and sisters around the world, including many Christian citizens of Muslim nations. Our *Ummah*, the solidarity of God's people in Islam, unites us together in our pain and in our joys. When the 1991 Gulf War started, we all identified with the Iraqis — not just the Arabs, but the Indonesians, the Pakistanis, and the Nigerians. Between the 1991 and 2003 Iraq wars, about 870,000 children died because of the shortage of antibiotics and because of malnutrition.[1] This was because of sanctions initiated by Western nations and imposed by the United Nations. Like you, I hated Saddam Hussein, but I ached for the Iraqis, and I still ache for them.

As he read this point he was passionate, and he meant every word.

8. I am amazed by the blind spot you have about your double standards. You are so focused on the war on terrorism that you are not aware of the huge battle that is being waged for our souls and minds as Muslims. We are being pulled in two directions: democracy on the one hand and fundamentalism on the other. The deciding factor for many of us is this: Which of the two, moderate Muslims or fundamentalists, will address more fairly the issue of the glaring injustice committed against the Palestinians?

No one in my extended family is a fundamentalist or a sympathizer with the fundamentalists. But since I came to your country and have seen with my own eyes your double standards, and as I use my intellect and see the glaring injustice, I am getting more and more attracted to fundamentalism. It feels like you are losing me.

If a young Jewish man leaves this country, goes to Israel, volunteers to serve with the Israeli army, and with his machine gun kills Palestinians as he occupies their land, you do not perceive him as a terrorist. No doubt this is because you see Israel as a democracy. I, on the other hand, see Israel as a state practicing racism as it is imposing an apartheid regime on the Palestinians in their land. If, on the other hand, a young Palestinian man who is an American citizen leaves this country and goes to Palestine and uses his only available weapon, his body, to defend his occupied territory, you perceive him as a terrorist. When you read in your Bible how Samson died, do you perceive him as a terrorist? Do you blame Samson for using his only available weapon, his body, to kill innocent civilians?

With this point his passion became even more intense. What he read sounded very personal because he was describing his agony as he was being pulled toward Islamic fundamentalism. He looked at me with eyes full of sorrow and anger when he said, "It feels like you are losing me." I knew that both of us, he and I, were thinking of the same person, even though neither of us mentioned him. Sayyid Qutb was an Egyptian international student who came to America as a cultural Muslim and while in America became a Muslim fundamentalist. He was hanged in Egypt in 1966, and yet his books continue to be a main source on Islamic fundamentalist theology.

9. Since 9/11, the way your U.S. administration has used the term *terrorist* has closed the minds of many to critical thinking. You describe terrorism as a cancer and therefore conclude, "We do not overanalyze the disease; we just kill it." The threat, you are told, is existential: "They want to destroy us. Therefore our only response can be to destroy them." Anyone who disagrees with these assumptions is said to be either naive, unpatriotic, an enemy, or cozying up to the terrorists.

In June/July of 2006, Israel wanted to punish *Hezbollah* for the kidnapping of two soldiers and for launching rockets on Israel. The issue did not start with the kidnapping of the two soldiers and the launching of rockets on Israel, however. The issue started in 1982, and before that in 1967, when the Sheb'a farms were occupied by Israel. As a Muslim, I was very angry with Hezbollah. They had no right to do what they did and drag their country, Lebanon, into disaster. But the way Israel responded shocked me. Israel did not limit its attacks to Hezbollah targets. It shredded Lebanon to pieces! Worse still, the U.S. administration approved of Israel's invasion, assuming that this would help create a new Middle East. What blows my mind is the blindness of your U.S. administration to the obvious. Do you think that the people of the Middle East can be bombed into democracy and terrorized into moderation?

I was astonished. Ahmad is a deep thinker with an international perspective, and he has the freedom to bash America even when he is in America.

10. In your politics and compassion you seem to be irrational in the way you identify with the Jews. I can never understand your logic. Jews today do not recognize Jesus as the Messiah. Their high priest, two thousand years ago, declared Him a blasphemer, and I think you believe that the Jews, along with the Romans, killed Jesus. On the other hand, we Muslims highly respect Him. We believe that Jesus was born of a virgin, healed the blind and those with leprosy, raised the dead, is now with God in heaven, and will come back on the Day of Judgment as the Sign of the Hour. Why do you feel theologically closer to the Jews than to the Muslims? I am not saying culturally; I am saying theologically. Of course you feel much closer culturally to the Jews than to us, the Muslims, because many Jews have a European background and many are citizens of the U.S. Again, my question is this: Why do you feel theologically closer to the Jews than to the Muslims?

I wondered how my American evangelical friends would respond to his question, "Why do you feel theologically closer to the Jews than to the Muslims?"

11. What I am going to say now might be very difficult for Christians to understand, but this is how Muslims feel. Please do not generalize and see all Muslims as evil. Evil is not in Islam or in Christianity as religions. Rather, it is in fanaticism. There are fanatics among Muslims, and there are fanatics among Christians. I am personally ashamed of the fanatics who are Muslims. How do you feel, as Christians, about Christian fundamentalist leaders who called the almighty God, the God we worship, a demon and who called our prophet Muhammad a terrorist and a "demon-possessed pedophile"? I am embarrassed and ashamed of the anti-Islamic drive behind the publication of the Danish cartoons in February 2006 and of the fanatical Muslim reaction to them. Please remember that the cartoons were perceived by many Muslims as "the straw that broke the

camel's back." I think the Muslims were trying to say to the Christian nations, "Enough is enough." Do you understand why it has become so easy for the fanatical Muslims to hijack and manipulate the Muslim crowds?

There was deep sorrow in his voice when he read this point. It felt like he was telling me that fanatics, on both sides, have hijacked Islam and Christianity.

12. As a Muslim it is very hard for me to separate church from state. In Islam this separation does not exist. So when you talk to me about Christianity, I understand that you want me to swallow the whole package: religion, politics, capitalism, and democracy. Sometimes we sense in you an attitude of victory when you come across with the attitude of surfing on a wave of power. Where is the humility and sense of justice that your Bible teaches? I love the passage in the Bible that one of you showed me: "With what shall I come before the LORD . . . ? Shall I come before him with burnt offerings . . . ? Will the LORD be pleased with thousands of rams . . . ? He has showed you, O man, what is good. And what does the LORD require of you? To act justly and to love mercy and to walk humbly with your God" (Micah 6:6-8). Like Gandhi, I am very much *attracted to* Christ *but not to your Christianity.*

I am sad that Gandhi was hampered by Christianity and by Christians in England. My fear is that we might lose Ahmad and many others like him if we continue to fail to distinguish between the gospel and our Western wrappings around the gospel.

When you try to convert me, I feel like you want to impose upon me your values. Back home, many Muslims who do not understand you like I do think that your strategy is, under the guise of freedom, to penetrate and destroy our culture, and especially our youth, with immorality and sex through your movies. Our values are very precious to us. We do not want to lose them as a result of globalization. Our values are primarily honor, loyalty, courage, politeness, passion for justice, generosity, hospitality, and fear of God.

What he is saying is true. I experienced many of these negative Western values during the years my family and I lived in Egypt. Muslims are really worried about the dangers that could come as a result of globalization.

## ME, THE RECEIVER

13. If I were to leave Islam and become integrated into Christianity, I would lose my authenticity among my own people. Not only would my people see me as a traitor, but I would have the same perception myself! I told you earlier that we judge not only on the basis of what is right versus what is wrong, but we judge even more on the basis of what is honorable versus what is shameful. Can you imagine the shame that my family and friends would feel if I were to leave Islam and get integrated into Christianity? I know that my parents would never tolerate that shame, but even if they did, they themselves would be shamed by our extended family and by all those who know us.

As I listened to him, I remembered the movie *Fiddler on the Roof* and thought about the great similarity between the Jews and the Muslims. In that movie, the Jewish milkman Tevye in Russia did not mind his eldest daughter marrying a poor Jewish tailor. He did not mind his second daughter marrying a young Jewish man who was an agnostic and a Communist. But when his third daughter married a Russian Christian, he never talked to her again.

14. If I converted to Christianity, my support system in life would be completely demolished. I would become, as it were, homeless and without family. How would I live? Are you able to provide for me a completely new support system?

My support system includes:

- Work that provides me with regular income. If I converted to Christianity, when I returned home to Egypt, I would lose my job and would end up unemployed. No Muslim would hire a traitor.
- My family, whom I belong to and who gives me roots, identity, and authenticity.
- My Muslim religious language that I feel at home with, and Muslim art, poetry, and music that I deeply appreciate.
- My Muslim proverbs, customs, and traditions.

*I do understand*, I thought to myself, *but there is another option that he is not thinking of.* (I'll address that in a later chapter.)

15. How can I give up my name, Ahmad, that was given to me when I was born and by which all my friends know me, and start being called Steve or Peter? How did you feel, as Americans, when you heard about the young American man, John Walker Lindh, who joined the Taliban in Afghanistan and took a Muslim name? By asking me to convert to Christianity, you are asking me to commit high treason.

Wow! Using John Walker Lindh as an example was powerful. I wondered how my Christian friends around the world would respond to this point. Further, I wondered how they would respond to the forcefulness of his whole argument.

That night, after Ahmad left, I lay in bed and thought about what he had revealed. There were a lot of questions in my mind. First, is there any truth in what he was saying? And if so, is there something I need to confess to God and ask forgiveness for from this man on behalf of my fellow citizens and fellow Christians? I thought of Nehemiah asking God to forgive him and the Jews in Jerusalem, even though he was living in Babylon and did not sin against God as his fellow countrymen did in Jerusalem. There were many more questions to consider. Furthermore, there was something very important that he shared with me about his father in Egypt.

In the next chapter, we will get into Ahmad's father's struggles and how both Ahmad and his dad perceive us as Western Christians.

## QUESTIONS FOR REFLECTION AND DISCUSSION

1. Has Ahmad stepped on your toes? If so, with which points?
2. In which of Ahmad's points do you find truth?
3. What would it take for you to step into Ahmad's shoes and try to see the world through his eyes?

# CHAPTER 3

# THEIR GRIEVANCES

It quickly became apparent to me that Ahmad does not see us the way we see ourselves. He has a different perspective on almost everything, such as current events, the history of the Middle East, the history of Christianity, and the history of Islam. When I determined to attempt to stand in his shoes and to see the world through his eyes, he was encouraged and felt safe with me. Before he left our home that evening, he told me that he had been able to visit his parents in Egypt a couple of times since he came to America. In one of his e-mails recently, he told me that during his last visit, in 2006, he was concerned about his dad, and he promised that he would send me a long, detailed e-mail about developments in Egypt and the Middle East through the eyes of his father. A few days later he sent me this e-mail:

## AHMAD'S FATHER

As you know, I moved to the United States just before 9/11, but I visited Egypt a couple of times in ensuing summers, and I cannot keep up with the changes that are taking place there. In my most recent visit to my family,

I spent a great deal of time with my father. He is a physician, semiretired, and Egyptian to the core. He is an avid reader, and these days he is into the Internet and is keeping up with current events. I have seen in him a growing frustration and an alarming change in his thinking. In the past he used to be very much against Islamic fundamentalism, but now he is more sympathetic with those views. He pointed out that as a result of the collapse of the Soviet Union and the first Gulf War in 1991, many developments took place in our country that are producing very rapid change. At one time there were two superpowers that served to maintain checks and balances. But since the collapse of the Soviet Union, and especially since 9/11, America's power seems to my father to have no restraints. Here is a brief summary of the thoughts that disturb him:

1. My father feels that his government is torn between pleasing America and pleasing its citizens who are highly influenced by the resurgence of Islam under the leadership of the Muslim Brotherhood. Deep within his soul he believes that the government of Egypt has lost its real independence and cannot make its own decisions.

2. The U.S. administration declared to our country, Egypt, and to the world right after 9/11 that all countries have to choose between two options in the war against terrorism: to be for the United States or to be against the United States—and America defines what that means. He feels that this is not fair because he does not see his country as one of the colonies of America. He thinks there should at least be a third option, which is choosing to be neutral when neutrality is the best choice from Egypt's point of view.

3. When my father watches TV with dish satellite capabilities, he is bombarded by new TV channels, started in the 1990s, that try to proselytize Muslims and convert them to Christianity. Not only that, but on some of these channels there are programs that blatantly attack Islam, the Qur'an, and Muhammad, and Egypt cannot do anything about it. He is often reminded by what Hasan al-Banna, the founder of the Muslim Brotherhood,

taught—that Christian missionaries paved the way to colonialism, and colonialism offered the umbrella of protection to missionaries to proselytize and attack Islam. Many of these programs are produced in the West or financed by Christians in the West. He is indignant but feels paralyzed.

4. He perceives that Western values differ from his Islamic Egyptian values. He recognizes that some of the Western values are good, but others allow for evil to penetrate the Egyptian society. He understands that freedom of expression is a high value in the West, but if there are no restraints, there is no limit to how far pornography, cults, and even Satan worship can spread among our people. He is very worried that as a result of globalization, the youth in our country will lose their fear of God and their respect for their parents and elders. He fears they will end up imitating the youth in the West in their music and movies. They could even end up with all sorts of addictions.

5. He would like for our country, Egypt, to have a choice in what to accept from the West and what to reject. Currently it looks like globalization does not allow for that.

6. As he looks at what is happening in the world, he sees that America, supported by Britain, is going on with its plans to solidify its political/military domination and its interests. Since oil is a powerful instrument of hegemony, he wonders if this is another form of modern colonialism. He wonders, *Is this neocolonialism?*

7. He is frustrated with the weakness of the United Nations and the growing strength of America as the only superpower. As an Egyptian he cannot vote for who should be president of the United States, and yet the U.S. president decides his destiny and the destiny of our country when it comes to major issues. The Iraqis did not vote for President Bush, nor did they vote for the war in Iraq. No wonder people in the Middle East are attracted to political terrorism, using violence to attract the attention of the world to their real or perceived grievances. This is the only way they can make their "vote" count and let the world know that their opinions matter.

8. In our extended family in Egypt, when conflicts arise, most of us tend to focus on resolving the conflicts. Some of us are known to be peacemakers. A few of us, through gossip and evil intentions, tend to add fuel to the conflicts. I think the same happens in international relationships. There are two outlooks:

1. Instigating conflicts by adding fuel to the fire
2. Resolving conflicts and being peacemakers

My father believes that America used to be a peacemaker at the time of President Carter, but since President George W. Bush, it has become an instigator of conflicts by adding fuel to the fire and by taking sides.

9. My father is not only concerned about Egypt but about the whole Middle East. The king of Jordan pleaded with President Bush not to wage war in Iraq, but President Bush would not listen. Now the Jordanians have more than one million Iraqi refugees, mostly in the capital, Amman, and they are increasing by the day. Are Americans aware of the impact of this influx of refugees on Jordan's schools, health services, housing, prostitution, crime, traffic, and so on? Jordan has a population of a little more than six million. Adding an additional one million is like America receiving fifty million refugees, mostly in New York City. America waged the war, but the Jordanians have to live with the consequences. Jordanians have to cooperate with America, or else the whole region will suffer as a result of a huge failure in Iraq. My father is not surprised at all by the increasing hatred toward America and by how easy it has become to recruit terrorists.

Wow, what an e-mail. Both Ahmad and his dad are stretching me and expanding my horizons by helping me see my blind spots. I have even started doubting some of my assumptions. One of my long-held assumptions has always been the value of Christianizing our culture, but I can feel the ground shifting beneath my feet.

## CHRISTENDOM VERSUS THE KINGDOM OF GOD

We all make assumptions, and most of the time we behave on the basis of these assumptions without being aware of them. Some of these assumptions harmonize with the teachings of the Bible, and others harmonize more with our culture. In what follows, I will begin addressing some of the assumptions that I have, or used to have.

There has been an evolution in our "Christian" history. In the beginning, those who believed in Christ were known as followers of the Way. In time, they were called Christians. In the fourth century, the emperor Constantine institutionalized Christianity, and it evolved into Christendom. The church entered into a "holy matrimony" with the state. In a later chapter I will go into more detail about the evolution of Christianity.

In contrast to Christendom, the kingdom of God has to do with:

- The invisible rule of God,
- The expansion of the gospel irrespective of who rules the land,
- Living with Christlike attitudes and behavior.

The kingdom of God has to do with the eternal rule of God, which is a present reality and one that will continue into the future. For Christians, our primary citizenship is the kingdom of God, not Christendom or Western culture.

Some of us Christians tend to confuse the kingdom of God with Christendom. Others of us assume that the kingdom of God overlaps with Christendom. In general, Christendom and democracies have been good because they have allowed those of us who are enjoying their benefits to choose our values and legislate our laws.* In many

---

* Perhaps a more accurate way of saying this is Christianity rather than Christendom as it refers to Christian values and culture. When I refer to Christendom, I am speaking about this aspect of Christianity. Christendom is associated with a specific place, like Europe, where Christianity is the official religion.

democratic nations where Christendom's values are flourishing, there is an "aspiration to preserve peace, to alleviate human suffering, to promote economic prosperity, freedom, human rights, and the rule of law."[1] In spite of these positives, the question needs to be asked: *Is Christendom absolutely essential for the survival of the kingdom of God and for the expansion of the gospel?* I used to assume that it was, but I am moving away from that position.

In 1682, a war was waged by the Ottoman Muslims against Austria, culminating in a siege of Vienna in the summer of 1683. The siege was broken, which resulted in a huge defeat of the Ottoman Muslims. The failure in Vienna was followed by a series of further defeats in Hungary and other parts of Europe. Following this catastrophic defeat of the Muslims, some European countries were energized to unite and form what was called the Holy League. The league impelled Russia to push the Turks farther south, and Russia reached the shores of the Black Sea. In January of 1699, with the help and mediation of the British and the Dutch, a peace treaty was signed between the Ottoman Empire and the Holy League at Carlowitz.

The peace treaty at Carlowitz became a landmark in history when once and for all Christendom defeated the Muslim empire and cut it down to size. Since that date, Christendom has been advancing and prospering, and Muslims have been, to a great extent, marginalized.

There is a fear today that another confrontation is taking place between Christendom and Islam. Many Christians today look back at the siege of Vienna in 1683 and see a repeat of the confrontation. If the Americans and the British are forced one day to retreat from Iraq, as the Soviets were forced to retreat from Afghanistan, it will embolden the Muslims, and it will be a huge defeat for Christendom. Not only the Americans and the Western world, but also most Christians around the world, agree that this is a situation that should be avoided at any cost. *The survival of Christendom seems a top priority for us.* But *is the survival of Christendom a top priority* for God?

At one time this was my assumption. But I started wondering about it and tried to imagine how God sees our world. If the Muslims would have been victorious in 1683, would that have been a defeat to God, to His kingdom, and to the expansion of the gospel? If the Ottomans had won that war, would God have panicked? Does God look at things the way we do? *Are we assuming that a defeat to Christendom is a defeat to God and to His kingdom? Do we assume that when Christians are in control, God is also in control?* Is it possible for the kingdom of God to expand and permeate the Muslims if the Christians are a minority and the Muslims are ruling the land? One of the sources on the kingdom of God is a controversial book by Gregory Boyd, *The Myth of a Christian Nation* (Zondervan). I will come to this book in one of the chapters of the addendum.

We can all agree that the state of Christendom in the United States is very strong. The Religious Right in America is a powerful force and could determine, to some extent, who will go to the White House, what laws will be passed, and which judges will be appointed to the Supreme Court. We can all agree also that the state of Christendom in China is very weak. The Communists control that nation, and many Christians are being persecuted because of their faith in Christ. Before Mao Tse-tung took over, Christians in the underground church in China were estimated to be close to one million. By the time he died, Christians in the underground persecuted church grew to about forty million. Is God rejoicing over the state of Christendom in America? Is He wringing His hands in worry as He panics about the weak state of Christendom in China? Are Christians around the world putting their efforts toward the preservation and expansion of democracy and Christendom and not focusing on God, living with Christlike attitudes, and the expansion of the gospel? *Are we preoccupied with the desire to protect, sustain, and empower Christendom?*

Politicians in democratic countries need to protect Christendom's values and advocate human rights. Living in democracy and protecting it is a necessary responsibility of the *politicians* because it is the best option in light of man's depravity and man's dignity. But we *Christians* are more than *politicians*. Christians need to go beyond the unifocal perspective and evaluate issues with a bifocal perspective. Our short-range perspective could be Christendom, but our long-range and more important perspective should be the kingdom of God, the beauty of Christ in our lives, and the expansion of the gospel. I yearn to see my Christian friends in Egypt enjoying the freedom that Christendom provides. I yearn to see Muslims around the world having the human right to worship God the way they choose. I yearn to see Muslim-background believers (MBBs) who are imprisoned in Muslim countries released and allowed to enjoy a life of freedom. I need to be careful, though, that I don't end up with shortsightedness and confuse the gospel's expansion with Christendom's expansion.

In his book *If You Want to Walk on Water, You've Got to Get out of the Boat*, John Ortberg described American Christians as people who prefer to stand in the shallow end of the swimming pool.[2] They like to be in control with their feet firmly on the floor. They do not like to go to the deep end and lose control. As they stay in the shallow end of the swimming pool, they tend to get bored, so they play with toys. In contrast, Christian minorities in many countries around the world are struggling for survival. Christendom in many of these countries is very weak, and the rights of Christians are ignored. Is God worried about Christendom in these countries? Of course He wants to protect His children and to bless them, and yet Christ prayed for His followers that God would not take them out of the world but that He would protect them from the Evil One. In essence, it is not a change of our circumstances that is important but rather our inner transformation in the midst of our circumstances.

A large Protestant church in Cairo, Egypt, has a prayer meeting every Monday evening. The meeting can go for two hours, and some people stay and pray all night. The number of those who attend the prayer meeting every Monday exceeds one thousand. They pray for their country, for the government in Egypt, and for the Arab world. Christendom is struggling in Egypt, but the kingdom of God is alive and well. In contrast, are Christians in the democratic nations of the world fighting hard for Christendom and for maintaining their position of control by demanding the right to stand in the shallow end of the swimming pool? Are we putting forth all our efforts and investing a great deal of sweat, blood, and tears into fighting for our rights to sustain and empower Christendom?* In our thinking, *do we align ourselves more with the emperor Constantine or with Jesus and the apostle Paul?*

During my years in Egypt (1975–1990), I experienced the alarming shrinking of Christendom in that country. Most, if not all, Christians, nominal and born-again, of all denominations, suffered to some extent or another. The fear of further shrinking of Christendom motivated many of the Christians to emigrate to the West. One of the obvious manifestations of the shrinking of Christendom was the call of the minaret, or the call to prayer.

Cairo has more than a thousand mosques. In addition, there are many improvised mosques that use the basements of high buildings as mosques. They place large loudspeakers on the tops of these buildings for the call of the minaret and for the Friday sermon. Muslims pray five times a day, and there is a call to prayer through the loudspeakers each time. To the Christian community in Egypt, the most painful call of the minaret is the sunrise call to prayer. I knew that, and I wanted to minister to my fellow believers in Christ to help them bring into captivity every thought to the obedience of Christ. One of the messages that I preached frequently in Egypt was based on 2 Corinthians 10:3-6.

---

* Our national interests and our way of life.

I used to illustrate practically how we can develop a new chain of thoughts made up of new links to replace the old chain of thoughts. So if I am one day at noon somewhere in Cairo and I hear the call of the minaret, the chain of my thoughts could go in this fashion:

1. This is the man who woke me up at five in the morning.
2. Do they have to use microphones? Whoever wants to rise up and pray at five can use his or her alarm clock.
3. Muslims are tightening the grip on Christianity, and they want to torment us and subdue us.
4. We need to demand our rights, but I do not know what we can do since they rule the land.
5. I hate them.
6. Lord, help me to love them.
7. Lord, help me to share the good news of the gospel with a Muslim in the coming week.

The last two links in the chain sound good, but I doubt whether God would answer them. Those two requests are motivated by guilt.

I have taught that we need to cut the chain after the first link, build a new chain, and practice thinking about it until it becomes our default mode. We cannot do anything about the first link in the chain because we will always hear the call of the minaret. Some of us might daydream about going at night to the top of the minaret, or to the top of the building where the speakers are, and cutting the electric wires connected to the huge speakers. But even if we did, they would reconnect the wires within the same day. So the new chain I recommended had the following links:

1. After hearing the call of the minaret, the thought that comes to mind is, *This is the man who woke me up at five in the morning.*

2. Thank You, Lord, that in Your wisdom and grace You planned for me to live in Egypt, which has a Muslim majority.

3. I wonder, Lord, about this man who is chanting the call to prayer. Is there someone in his family who is sick, or is his family struggling with any issues?

4. Lord, somehow help this man and his family to realize how much You love them.

5. Lord, help me to see Muslims through Your eyes.

6. Lord, help me to love them.

7. Lord, help me to share the good news of the gospel with a Muslim in the coming week.

The last two links on this new chain of thoughts are identical to the last two links on the first chain. But in the second chain, the last two links are motivated by love and compassion rather than by guilt.

It was relatively easy for me to preach this message because there were no mosques close to our apartment. We could hear the call to prayer in the distance from two mosques, but they were not close enough to wake me up at sunrise. But things changed suddenly.

Without our knowing it, the ground floor in a tall building about seventy meters from our apartment was transformed into a mosque, and a huge loudspeaker was placed on top of that building. The first call to prayer was early one morning on a cold winter day. It started so suddenly and loudly that I almost fell out of bed. The noise was unbearable due to the volume and to the loud echo that ensued because the speaker was facing a tall building in front of our apartment. My Christendom was so shrunk that I pleaded to God for mercy. It was unbearable. Whatever I preached on 2 Corinthians 10:3-6 about the need to transform my thinking patterns evaporated and became irrelevant. We pleaded to God for mercy on that day, and God answered our prayers within a few hours. They changed the direction of the speaker to face us directly. It became a bit louder, but there was no more echo. That was the mercy of God.

Every morning at sunrise we would wake up with the man clearing his throat before he started to chant the call to prayer. The sentences that make up the call to prayer are as follows:

1. God is great/transcendent.
2. There is no God but God.
3. Muhammad is the messenger of God.
4. Arise and pray.
5. Arise and do good works.
6. God is great/transcendent.
7. There is no God but God.

I found myself every morning praying with our neighbor, the man on the loudspeaker at the mosque next door. Some verses came to mind when he addressed God's greatness and transcendence. Deuteronomy 6:4-5 came to mind when he called out God's oneness: "The LORD our God, the LORD is one. Love the LORD your God with all your heart and with all your soul and with all your strength." My biggest struggle came from the two introductory phrases that he said every morning before he started to chant the dawn call to prayer. After clearing his throat (that was enough to wake me up), our neighbor would say, "Get up and pray. To pray is better than to sleep." It was cold, and I felt guilty that I was too lazy and cold to get out of bed and pray. I asked God to forgive me, and I prayed as I was covered with my warm blankets. I thanked God for the faithfulness and zeal of this man and for his desire not only to get up but to leave his apartment and go to the mosque.

Sunrise prayer at five in the morning became my daily practice. At times I would go back to sleep after the call to prayer, and at other times I would start my day. A few weeks into it, I experienced an amazing miracle. Loud as it was, I sometimes found myself going back to sleep even before the man finished chanting the call to prayer.

It is easy to long for an enlarged Christendom because when we are standing in the shallow end of the swimming pool, it feels good to be in control. We are standing upright, and our feet feel the floor of the pool. In my experience with our neighboring mosque in Egypt, God forced me out into the deep end of the pool, where I lost control but learned to swim. This is a lesson that I learned then and will continue to learn and relearn for the rest of my life.

## HINDERED BY THE MESSENGER

I had a deep yearning to share the gospel in depth with Ahmad. He is conservative in his theology, yet his attitude is very open-minded. If not for his open-mindedness, he would not have connected with Americans. He would not have persisted in refusing to be absorbed by the Muslim association at the university. He shared with me that so many American Christians whom he came to love were driven to speak and not to listen. They were not that interested in listening to his perspective. They did a great deal of talking about Christ and were surprised that he did not accept their logic of his need to convert to Christianity.

Ahmad told me,

They did not realize they needed to allow me to air my anguish before I could listen. I could not listen to their message because I was hindered by them, the messengers. Sometimes when I interrupted them and tried to speak out on issues that are important to me, they were caught by surprise. They wondered why I would be concerned about the Crusades that took place centuries ago. They were amazed at how I see colonialism continuing today in various forms. They were shocked by my views on Israel and its history. They assumed that there is only one true history of Israel, and it is the history that they learned in their churches and in some of their Christian books. They could understand why I was irritated by some TV evangelists, but they assumed that Christians around the world should be biased in favor of Israel and against all the Arabs and all the Muslims around the world.

I went back to Ahmad's presentation and looked more carefully at the issues he raised under the category "You, the Messenger." The first of his issues was the Crusades.

## THE CRUSADES

In his presentation of the Muslims' worldview, Ahmad said,

The Crusades took place in the twelfth and thirteenth centuries. Wave after wave of armies kept coming to invade our lands for two hundred years. Western Christian countries sent their armies to Jerusalem to force upon Muslims a Christian jihad or "holy war" to clean up Jerusalem. Jerusalem is a city that is very special, not only to you, but to us, too. Sir Steven Runciman, your famous historian of the Crusades, said, "It was this blood-thirsty Christian fanaticism . . . that recreated the fanaticism of Islam." In your current U.S. Middle East policy, are you fueling and strengthening fanaticism within Islam? *In your neo-Crusader attitude, have you unleashed Islamic fanaticism and escalated violence?* In your desire to impose U.S.-style democracy on the Middle East, have you opened up a can of worms of Islamic fundamentalism?

As I thought about the Crusades, I wondered why he blames me, a Protestant, for something done by the Catholics centuries ago. I came to the realization right away that he does not distinguish between Catholics and Protestants. He sees us all as Christians. I thought, *Why doesn't he forgive and forget? How many centuries will it take Muslims to get over this?* Then I realized as I looked at history and current events from their perspective, they do not see the Crusades as merely events that took place centuries ago. They see a Crusader attitude that continues today, and that is the reason they are not able to heal, forgive, and forget.*

## NEOCOLONIALISM

I next reviewed Ahmad's presentation regarding colonialism. Here is what he had to say:

Every Muslim country in the world, except Iran, Turkey, Saudi Arabia, and Yemen, has been colonized by Western Christian nations such as Portugal, Britain, France, and Holland. These Western Christian countries came and depleted our natural resources. Under the guise of wanting to civilize us and introduce democracy, they wished to impose upon us Muslims an inferior status. Some of our Muslim leaders wonder, *Is this same colonialism continuing today under a different name?* If the war in Iraq and its aftermath go your way, what kind of control will you exercise over Iraq and its neighbors?

---

\* For readers who want to explore the addendum after reading this book, there are eight chapters. These chapters are summaries of books to whet your appetite and to motivate you to read books that adequately address these issues from the Muslim perspective. Some of these chapters in the addendum will be updated to keep up with current events. Chapter 2 of the addendum summarizes the important work of Fred Wright on the Crusades.

As I thought about his statement, I was somewhat intrigued by how he connected the Iraq war with colonialism. It is true that Christendom practiced colonialism in its long history, but I thought colonialism was completely finished.

I found the book *Transforming Mission* by David Bosch[3] to be a great source in providing me with the historical roots for colonialism. It also showed me something about our church history that I was not eager to know. I was amazed by the links that colonialism had to some passages in the Bible. I learned about Augustine and those who followed him in paving the way for colonialism. Also, as I looked at Professor Rashid Khalidi's books, I came to see that neocolonialism is a reality that is continuing today under different names.[4]

## ISRAEL

Ahmad went on to say,

Since the creation of Israel in 1948, and the events that led to it, Israel has been a thorn in our side. Before that time Muslims did not have a big problem with Jews. Those responsible for the Spanish Inquisition and the Holocaust came from a Christian background, not a Muslim background!

In a private conversation with Ahmad, he told me,

Whenever I read in Arabic the modern history of Israel and Palestine, I can tell there is a bias in our history books toward the Palestinians and against the Jews. Now when I read the same history written by Americans and Europeans I find there is also a bias, but in the opposite direction. Are people in the West aware of their bias?

Israel is a hot issue to Ahmad. I found out that if I am willing to listen and attempt to understand his perspective, it contributes to strengthening a bridge of relationship between us. I believe that the stronger the bridge, the heavier the truth it can carry. I do not have to agree with Ahmad on all issues, but I can listen to him because I want to stand in his shoes and see the world through his eyes. Ahmad is not a Palestinian; he is an Egyptian. Yet it is amazing how emotionally involved he is with the Palestinian issue.

Chapter 4 in the addendum deals with "The Other Side of the Coin on the History of Israel and Palestine" and chapter 5 deals with "Rashid Khalidi on the History of Israel and Palestine." In these two treatments, I only scratch the surface as I attempt to summarize the ideas of Colin Chapman and Professor Khalidi. I hope that these two chapters will motivate you to get into the books of these two men. Colin Chapman is a man of God who has taught at seminaries in several countries in the Middle East and Britain. He has authored many books, and he is an authority on this topic. Dr. Khalidi is the chair of Middle Eastern Studies at Columbia University. Reading his ideas helped me balance what I learned from Professor Bernard Lewis* and helped me see the history of the Middle East through the eyes of an Arab Muslim American.

Another resource on this subject is President Carter's book *Palestine: Peace Not Apartheid.* President Carter is a trusted and respected American president in the eyes of Muslims. He is known as a peacemaker, and he was able to bring peace between Israel and Egypt. He continues to make an impact on the world through his various humanitarian efforts and his monitoring of free elections.

---

\*  Professor Bernard Lewis was one of the main advisers to the Bush administration on how to deal with Muslims in the Middle East. According to *Time* magazine, following the Iraq war he was considered one of the most influential people in the world because his theory was adopted by the Bush administration and was a motivation for going to war with Iraq. One of the famous books by Professor Lewis is *What Went Wrong? The Clash Between Islam and Modernity in the Middle East* (Harper Perennial, 2003).

## ESCHATOLOGY

In a private conversation with Ahmad, he told me,

I do not see much difference between some Shi'ites in Iran who are waiting for the Hidden *Imam* and Christian Zionist preachers on American TV. They both seem to believe that they can speed up the appearance of the Hidden Imam or the return of Christ.*

This is another very hot issue for evangelicals and for Muslims. Some evangelicals feel very strongly about Israel because they view current events in light of what they see as the clock ticking in preparation for the coming of Christ. Ahmad, on the other hand, sees the eschatology of Iran's leader, Mahmoud Ahmadinejad, as similar to that of some TV evangelists in America.

I hope the addendum's chapter 6 titled "Chapman and Others on Eschatology" will motivate you to look at eschatology with different eyes for the sake of Ahmad and people like him. People like Ahmad do not see Jesus; they see Him wrapped with an eschatology that does not make sense to them. Are we able to present Jesus without our wrappings around Him so that the Muslims can see Him rather than being tripped up by us, His messengers?

---

\* The core of the Shi'ite religious worldview is the Hidden Imam. While the stories of the first eleven Imams are historical in nature, the history of the twelfth Imam is mystical and miraculous. The central Shi'ite doctrines revolving around the Hidden Imam are the doctrines of Occultation and Return. The doctrine of Occultation is simply the belief that God hid Muhammed al-Mahdi away from the eyes of men in order to preserve his life. God has miraculously kept him alive since the day he was hidden in 874. Eventually God will reveal al-Mahdi to the world, and he will return to guide humanity.

## CHRISTENDOM AND ISLAM

In the addendum I have included a chapter with the title "The Threat of a Holy World War." Since 9/11, there has been a steady and growing separation between Christendom and the Muslim world. It looks as though we are coming to an open confrontation with the Muslims similar to the siege of Vienna in 1683. Who is going to win the war? At what cost and for what stakes? Are we occupied with Christendom at the cost of the kingdom of God and the expansion of the gospel? In this chapter I've tried to share my heart and some of my concerns about what is happening in our world today.

In the next chapter, we will look at the Muslims' worldview from a Muslim woman's perspective, and in the rest of the book we will unpack and address the issues that Ahmad raised in his presentation.

## QUESTIONS FOR REFLECTION AND DISCUSSION

1. Are the concerns of Ahmad's father legitimate? Which ones? Consider each concern one by one. Do you sympathize with Ahmad's father?

2. Is Christendom or western civilization essential to the survival of the kingdom of God and for the expansion of the Gospel? Is the survival of western civilization a top priority for God? Should it be a top priority for Christians?

3. Which scenario sounds most appealing to you: Living as an Iranian follower of Christ and being part of the exploding church in Iran or living as an easy-going Christian in the United States?

4. Are western Christians preoccupied with the desire to protect, sustain, and empower Christendom or western civilization? Is our thinking more aligned with the emperor

Augustine or with Jesus and the apostle Paul?

5. Ahmad observed that many American Christians whom he came to love were driven to speak about Christ but not to listen. Is there truth in his observation about Christians in general?

6. Does the additional information offered in the Addendum to this book interest you? What specifically are you most curious about?

# CHAPTER 4

# AHMAD'S SISTER

In the previous three chapters, I introduced you to my friend Ahmad and his father. In this chapter, I would like to introduce you to Ahmad's sister and mother. In the course of my discussion, I will also need to speak more about Ahmad's father.

I once asked Ahmad if there were many differences between the views of Muslim women and men regarding the issues he raised. He told me that the issues are generic and apply across gender but of course women have a distinct perspective. So I asked him whether his sister would be willing to make a contribution about the Muslim woman's worldview, and he promised he would ask her. A few weeks later, I received an e-mail from Ahmad with an attachment containing his sister's response to my request.

Fatima and her mother in this chapter are fictitious, but she and her worldview are a composite of real people I know or whose writings I have read. What follows is the substance of an e-mail attachment from Fatima.

## FATIMA AND HER PARENTS

My name is Fatima Abdul Mun'im, and I am glad that both my brother and my father encouraged me to make my contribution. I do have a contribution to make about our worldview from my unique perspective as an educated Muslim woman. I fully agree with all that my father and brother have communicated about our worldview.

Before I get into sharing about myself and my views, however, I would like to introduce my mother. Although she is not as educated as the rest of us in our family since she has only a high school diploma, her wisdom is not limited to her schooling. She has continued over the years to grow and mature.

In some ways my mother is the power behind my dad. She loves him and our family on a daily basis. With her servant heart and stable personality, she has been a pillar of strength to my dad, to Ahmad, and to me. Both Ahmad and I drifted away from God and from some of our values in our teen years. But day in and day out my mother prayed for us, believed in us, and instilled within us the fear of God.

In Islam we have two types of prayer that we call in Arabic *salat* and *du'aa*. Salat is the ceremonial prayer that should be practiced five times a day, while du'aa is the spontaneous prayer that believers lift up to God during the day while being busy living their lives. My mother practiced that spontaneous prayer for us over the years, and we are who we are because God answered her prayers. I will never forget that early morning when I was still a child and I got up to use the toilet. It was still dark, and there she was on her knees with her head covered, praying the sunrise salat prayer. She didn't see me, but her example left a permanent impression on my life.

I could say much more about my mother, but now I need to introduce myself. I am Ahmad's sister, Fatima. In Egypt-spoken Arabic, they call me Fatma. I am proud of both my first name and my family name. Fatima was the name of the daughter of the prophet Muhammad. She was also the wife of Ali, the fourth caliph. My family name is Abdul Mun'im, and it means "the servant of the Gracious God."

I have a master's degree in physics, and I teach at the American University of Cairo. AUC is a university that follows the American educational system, and the credits are transferable to American universities. Someday I would like to go to graduate school and study for a PhD, perhaps in England rather than in the States. I teach male and female students, and I am not that much older than some of my students. I work with and relate daily to male and female colleagues, most of whom are Egyptians; a few are Americans and Europeans.

I love my city, Cairo, where I have lived all my life. I love our culture and our people, though I am worn out by our crowded streets and stressful traffic. I struggle with the daily challenge of finding a place to park my car in the morning near the university and in the evening near our apartment. There is a great deal of pollution in Cairo, and the streets are filthy. In spite of all these things, I would rather live in Cairo than anywhere else in the world. In our obvious bias we say, *"Masr um dunya,"* which means, "Egypt gave birth to the world."

I read what Ahmad has written describing our Muslim worldview. I have not been to America, but I know many Americans at our university, both colleagues and students. Furthermore, I am into the Internet, and I keep up with current events. I liked the way my brother addressed our issues under three categories: the message of the Western Christians, the Western Christians themselves, and why it is unthinkable for us to give up our culture in order to adopt the European or American culture and become Christians. We are people with deep roots in a civilization that goes back at least five thousand years. Why should we be uprooted from our families, our culture, and our natural place of belongingness? Yes, I fully agree with what my brother, Ahmad, has communicated.

As for my father, he is one of my heroes. He is a very respected physician, though he is now semiretired. His patients love him, and his friends and colleagues respect him. I have seen in him over the years the firmness and, at the same time, the gentleness that make him a great father. He has always treated me with dignity, just as he treated Ahmad with dignity. There are not many fathers like mine, and several of my female friends envy me for my family. I hope that I will be lucky and marry a husband with a character similar to my father's.

Over the past few years, all of us in our family have observed a growing concern that my father has about the future of our country. In the past he never sympathized with the fundamentalists. But since the Gulf War in 1991, and especially since 9/11, we have seen in him an obvious change and a growing sympathy with the fundamentalists' concerns. In the past he repeatedly wrote articles in our newspapers criticizing Islamic fundamentalism and the fundamentalists. He even received death threats from some of the fanatical Muslims, but that did not deter him from expressing his opinions in public. He also wrote an article in one of our newspapers critiquing Christian fundamentalism in America and wondered why Christians in the West are not critical of their own fundamentalism. He is still not at all sympathetic with the theology of Islamic fundamentalism, but he is now attracted to their pursuit of justice, their courage in facing America, and their refusal to become puppets of the West.

I read the points that my father contributed to Ahmad's description of our worldview. I fully agree with my father about the concerns that disturb him.

## Fatima's Contribution

Many people in the West paint us with a broad brush and assume that all Muslims are fundamentalists or fanatics. Much of the Western media presents us as a monolithic entity, ignoring our diversity. We are more than one billion people. We live on all continents and speak a great variety of languages. Among us are the orthodox, the ambivalent, the contented, the secular, the mystic, the fundamentalist, and the folk Muslim. I am sad to say that many of us live in poverty and believe in superstitions.

Many people in the West assume that there is no place for women in Muslim societies. They think that all women live in the shadow of men with no independent existence. They tend to forget that Indonesia had a female president and Pakistan had a female prime minister. Indonesia and Pakistan are Muslim countries with huge populations.

It is true that many of the Muslim women in the world are abused and are suppressed by their male relatives. Sadly, those Muslim male relatives abuse our doctrines to manipulate and control women. This phenomenon is true not only of Muslims but of Christians and Jews as well. Ahmad, my brother, told me that some of the churches in America that he visited do not allow women to hold leadership offices. As for Jews and their religion, from what I know about the Old Testament, polygamy was permitted. King Solomon had wives and mistresses in the hundreds. For my part, I am embarrassed and ashamed by the Muslim women who live in ignorance, subservience, and dependency. I long for our Muslim women to catch up and start living in the twenty-first century.

Here are a few issues I would like to add to what my brother and father shared. They will be my unique contribution as an educated Muslim woman.

## MODESTY AND WEARING THE HIJAB

For most of my life I have observed the fast of Ramadan, but not every single day of the month. Recently, I have been more faithful to observe the fast during the whole month of Ramadan. A few years ago, I also decided to start wearing the *hijab*. The hijab is a head cover for women that covers the hair but does not cover the face. When some of my friends at the university saw me wearing the hijab for the first time, they wondered whether

I was beginning to lean toward fundamentalism. Far from it. I wanted to start wearing the hijab to make a statement. I wanted to communicate that I am a spiritual woman and that I do not want my femininity to be a stumbling block to my male students and colleagues at the university.

Nobody in my family asked me to wear the hijab. I do not feel oppressed as I wear it. On the contrary, I feel empowered. I communicate the message that I am not cheap or sexually available. I take pride in our Muslim heritage and culture. I do not want to get associated with Western secularism. I do not want to be treated as a sexual object. At the same time, I do not want to wear the *niqab*, which is used by Muslim fundamentalist women and shows only their eyes. I do not want to be associated with them either. I want to convey that I am intelligent and can cope well with the challenges that our world offers. I am living in the world, but I do not want to become worldly.

It is a challenge for us Muslim women to convey our beauty in a modest manner. Our beauty can be manifested in the face and should spring from inside the personality. The outer beauty should be manifested by a sense of security, maturity, and human dignity rather than by sensuality. Sex is a private matter for us, and virginity needs to be preserved till marriage.

Our attractiveness must be sophisticated in nature so that we will not be seductive. I do not like the pressure that the advertising agencies in the West place upon Western women. The message I see in Western advertising is that for a woman to be powerful, she must also be sexy. No wonder Western women suffer with pressures that lead to teenage pregnancies, anorexia, sexually transmitted diseases, cohabitation, and breast implants. I think it would be wrong for Muslim women to use their femininity to manipulate and create a place for themselves in the workplace. They cheapen themselves if they resort to such techniques.

When it comes to dating and getting married, as a teenager I used to think that falling in love was the condition for the right marriage. Now as I have grown older and see life in a more mature manner, I believe that whoever falls in love will, sooner or later, fall out of love. Commitment, rather than falling in love, should be the basis for getting married. I would like my parents to play a role in my marriage. Arranged marriages are highly valued in our culture.

A Muslim woman marries a man who is not extracted from his family but is highly connected with his extended family. There should be compatibility not only between the two partners but also between the two families. When our Muslim marriages come under strain, there is support and counsel from both families. Our families are nuclear families, which are vitally connected to the extended families. We experience a sense of belongingness. When I get married and have children, I would like to stay at home for a few years to raise my children, depending on whether my future husband can earn enough money for us to survive. Staying at home and raising children does not diminish me as a woman. On the contrary, I will be contributing to raising the next generation to grow up with maturity and fear of God.

The university might not give me the option of having a home leave without losing my job. In that case I am not abandoned. My extended family, and especially my mother, will help me raise my children. I highly respect my mother for what she did in raising us. Her value is not in having a job outside the house but in knowing who she is and what she is called to do.

Perhaps I am idealistic in my expectations about my future. My optimism comes from the fact that I belong to a great family. Many Muslim women cannot attain the kind of job I have, nor do many have my bright dreams for the future.

As you see, Islam is not only a theology. For us, Islam is a culture, a worldview, and a way of life. But what about the Qur'an? What does it teach about women?[1]

## THE PLACE OF WOMEN IN THE QUR'AN

There is a great deal of diversity within Islam when it comes to inter-pretations of the Qur'an. That is why we have different sects and dif-ferent schools of jurisprudence. I guess the same diversity exists within Christianity as well. I do not see myself as a traditional Muslim or a Muslim fundamentalist, but I see myself as a *progressive, educated Muslim woman with deep roots in Islamic culture.* I like to see myself as *deeply rooted in Islam* and at the same time as *an open-minded* Muslim woman who is living in the twenty-first century.

Personally, I believe that all the Qur'anic passages were revealed in a specific time and context in history. Furthermore, they were revealed in general or particular circumstances. Therefore, the message of a Qur'anic text should be perceived in light of that historical context and in light of the *spirit of the Qur'an*, rather than in the literal interpretation of that text.

Some passages served their purposes primarily at the time of the prophet, while other passages continue to be relevant today. The litmus test from my point of view is the *spirit of the Qur'an.* For instance, polygamy in Islam was encouraged at the time of the prophet to deal with a historical situation. Many men were getting killed in battles and as a result there were many widows. These widows were potentially forced into poverty or prostitution. So God in His mercy revealed to our prophet in the teach-ings of the Qur'an the practice of polygamy. This practice was based on mercy so that widows would have financial and emotional security and a place of belongingness. Some traditional Muslim men abuse the Qur'an by wanting to marry several wives to satisfy their lust and their sexual desires. In the process, they disobey the *spirit of the Qur'an* by practicing polygamy not for the sake of mercy and love, but rather for selfishness and self-gratification.

Some traditional Muslim men assume that Islam teaches that women are weak, inferior, inherently evil, intellectually incapable, and spiritually lacking. Whatever comes close to this in the Qur'an and *Hadith* (life and teaching of the prophet) must have been addressing a particular situation at the time of the prophet and is no longer relevant. It is unfortunate that historically, Muslim women always lived in a male-oriented society in which the men monopolized the right to interpret the Qur'an. And it is a sad reality that women as a whole possess 1/1000 of the wealth of the world despite the fact that they comprise 50 percent of the world's population. This injustice reveals the fact that God is not reigning in these societies. I believe this applies to all religions. Violence, oppression, injustice, and despotism are deviations from the true religion, and they should be confronted. Islam, in spirit, is a religion that is compatible with human nature and if practiced correctly should bring about justice and equality.

Unlike Christianity's version, in the Qur'an's story of the Fall, Eve was not the sole cause. Both Adam and Eve were tempted, neither heeded the warning, and therefore the Fall occurred. In the same way that guilt is distributed evenly, the Qur'an offers equal opportunities to men and women: "Men should have a portion of whatever they have earned, while women should have a portion of whatever they have earned" (Surah 4:32).

When it comes to inheritance, according to Surah 4:11, the son has the right to two-thirds and the daughter has the right to only one-third. Is that unjust? It appears so, but when we look at its context we find that the share of the daughter is for her use only. While the share of the man has two parts, one third is for his personal use and the other third is to be spent on his wife and children. The son gets an extra share so that he can provide for his family.

When we look at the spiritual capacities and requirements of men and women in the Qur'an, we see equality and no differentiation in gender. The Qur'an clearly teaches that

Muslim men and Muslim women, believing men and believing women, devout men and devout women, truthful men and truthful women, patient men and patient women, reverent men and reverent women, charitable men and charitable women, fasting men and fasting women, and men who safeguard their private parts and women who safeguard [theirs], and men who remember God often and women who remember [Him]—for [all of] them God has prepared forgiveness and a splendid wage. (Surah 33:35)

There are no distinctions between men and women as they seek to live according to the teaching of the Qur'an: "The ones who believe and perform honorable deeds"—be they male or female—"will have gardens of Bliss to live in for ever" (Surah 31:8).

In relating to parents, the Qur'an teaches both men and women to honor their parents: "[Show] kindness to your parents. . . . Protect them carefully from outsiders, and SAY: 'My Lord, show them mercy, just as they cared for me [when I was] a little child!'" (Surah 17:23-24). The requirement is of both sons and daughters, and the respect is due to both father and mother.

So what has happened in the history of Islam? After the death of our prophet, there was a reemergence of the patriarchal society. Religion was used to justify the norms of the tribe. Rather than Islam transforming tribal society, the sad reality is that Islam was manipulated by the tribal patriarchal system. Early Islam shows us that during the life of the prophet and right after his death, there were powerful and able women.[2]

## MUSLIM WOMEN

Here are three illustrations of women in our early history who demonstrate what women were like.

# KHADIJAH

Khadijah was the first wife of the prophet. As long as she was alive, the prophet did not marry any other wives. Before marrying the prophet, she was a rich widow of independent means. She had her own business, and at one time in his youth Muhammad was employed by her. When it came to their marriage, she took the initiative and sent him a proposal of marriage. So she was independent, assertive, and did not conform to the image of women who were passive and subservient. She was fifteen years older than the prophet, and she was given the title "the mother of all believers."

# FATIMA

Fatima was the daughter of the prophet. She saw her father being persecuted because of his faith in the One God during the Mecca stage, and she stood by him and encouraged him. She was an example in endurance and perseverance in the midst of difficult circumstances. After the death of her father and her marriage to Ali, she had the political courage to disagree with the decision of the Muslim majority, who chose Abu Bakr as the first caliph when in her view it should have been Ali's right to be the first caliph. She maintained a political role of opposition until her death. Fatima was known as the daughter of the prophet; the wife of Ali, the fourth caliph; and the mother of the grandsons of the prophet. She had a major role in our history, and I am proud to carry her name.

# 'AISHAH

'Aishah was one of the wives of the prophet. She was a politically astute woman who had a major role to play after the death of the prophet. She was a main source for our Muslim tradition that speaks about the life and teachings of the prophet Muhammad. So much of what is considered as reliable texts in the Hadith came from 'Aishah as the primary source. She was a bold woman. Not only did she make her views known, but when she was opposed, she went to the battlefield to fight against the wrongs that were committed.

The plight of Muslim women today is not because of our religion but because our religion got manipulated by patriarchal societies. The Qur'an gives a testimony and an acceptance to women ruling: "I found a woman ruling over them, and she has been given everything and has a splendid throne" (Surah 27:23).

This is my contribution to what my brother and my father described as our Muslim worldview.

» » »

As I read Fatima's e-mail—forwarded to me by Ahmad—I had a deeper respect not only for him but also for his whole family. I felt deep compassion for them and for the many others like them.

## QUESTIONS FOR REFLECTION AND DISCUSSION

1. Fatima presented a liberal Islamic perspective. What did you think of it?
2. What did you think of Fatima's way of thinking and her values?
3. Has Fatima helped you see another face of Islam and Muslims? How would you describe it?

CHAPTER 5

# THE DRIVING FORCE
# OF ASSUMPTIONS

*There is only one set of true assumptions, the biblical assumptions.*

— A Singaporean Christian

In one of our conversations, Ahmad told me, *"It seems you have your assumptions and we, as Muslims, have our assumptions. If we can become aware of both sets of assumptions, then I think we can begin to understand one another."*

Every January, I teach a one-week course on "Islam in the Twenty-First Century" at Columbia International University. One of my students who keeps me informed about websites and articles sent me a questionable website (MEMRI: The Middle East Media Research Institute at http://memritv.org/) that I looked at. I wanted to know the pulse of the Iraqi Muslims by watching video summaries of sermons preached in mosques on Fridays in their country. The sermons are in Arabic, and there are subtitles in English. I was shocked by how bluntly they preached against Israel and America and how they prayed that God would pour out His wrath on both countries. It helped me to watch and listen to what Muslims hear in packed mosques every Friday.

In contrast, on March 21, 2006, Al Jazeera satellite TV aired a live debate between a Muslim scholar and an Arab lady, Dr. Wafa Sultan, who now resides in the United States. The show on Al Jazeera is called "The Other Viewpoint" and is by far the most watched TV show in the Arab world. This video was available in a summary form and with English subtitles on the same website mentioned above (MEMRI). Dr. Sultan comes from Syria and is from a Muslim background. She calls herself a secular person, an atheist, who does not believe in the supernatural. She made a vehement attack on Islam and Muslims and accused them of barbarism.

Many people in the West assume that the biggest war in the world today is the war on terrorism. I believe that there is a *much bigger and more important war*, with more dangerous consequences for the whole world and the mobility of the gospel for many years to come. The longer we wait to address this huge war, the more difficult it will be for us to deal with it. This war is not against Muslims but *within Islam itself* as the two stories I mentioned above demonstrate. I will come back to this war later on in this chapter.

## CITIZENS OF THE KINGDOM

Throughout this book, I will be sharing assumptions that are open to challenge in light of what the Bible teaches and in light of a good understanding of Muslims and their worldview. We all make assumptions. The challenge for us is to identify our assumptions and look at them through the lens of the Scriptures and the lens of the Muslims' worldview. One assumption that I have already made is that *our primary loyalty is to the expansion of the gospel among the nations, and our primary citizenship is in the kingdom of God rather than in Christendom.*

Do you remember what I shared with the Sunday school class in 1991 when we evaluated the first Gulf War, not as Iraqi Muslims nor as redneck Americans, but as Christians who are Americans? Rick Warren, in his book *The Purpose Driven Life* (in the chapter "Life Is a Temporary Assignment") reminded us that the Bible teaches that life, compared with eternity, is extremely brief. It is a temporary residence. The Bible describes it as a mist that appears very briefly and then vanishes. Pastor Warren wrote,

> Imagine if you were asked by your country to be an ambassador to an enemy nation. You would probably have to learn a new language and adapt to some customs and cultural differences in order to be polite and to accomplish your mission. As an ambassador, you would not be able to isolate yourself from the enemy. To fulfill your mission, you would have to contact and relate to them. But suppose you became so comfortable with this foreign country that you fell in love with it, preferring it to your homeland. Your loyalty and commitment would change. Your role as ambassador would be compromised. Instead of representing your home country, you would start acting like the enemy. You'd be a traitor.[1]

In light of this assumption, how do I perceive and relate to Muslim-background believers in Christ? There are increasing numbers of new believers in Christ from Muslim backgrounds who do not speak my language and are not from my race or my country. Do I see them as my brothers and sisters and desire to connect with them and pray for them? Or is my loyalty greater to socially and politically hyperconservative fellow citizens who agree with my conservative politics but show no desire to live for Christ?

## THE MODERATES VERSUS THE FANATICS

Another assumption I have is that *open-minded Muslims are more open to the gospel than fanatics.*

One of my brothers in Christ looks like Osama bin Laden and used to have a theology similar to that of bin Laden. Yet he is an example of what I mean by *the open-minded Muslims.* At a certain stage in my friend's journey, with genuine honesty, he tried to find answers to some tough theological issues in Islam. This led him to a stage of doubt that was followed by a search for God in the New Testament. Finally he came to know Christ. In April 2005 he got arrested and was imprisoned. His wife was able to visit him for the first time three months later. He continued to be imprisoned for his faith in Christ for two full years, which is illegal. He was in solitary confinement in a prison underground, living with unbearable circumstances. As a result of his deep commitment, he paid a high cost to follow his new Lord Jesus Christ. He was told by those who arrested him that he would never be released unless he committed himself to become an informer about other Muslims who have become followers of Christ. He refused that offer and paid for it for two years.

I differentiate between the *fundamentalists* and the *fanatics.* The *fundamentalists* are committed Muslims who are going back to the literal fundamentals of their faith and are deeply committed and willing to pay any cost to follow God. They are driven by *theology* and by *deep commitment.* Paul described his past in Philippians 3 as a Jewish militant fundamentalist. After his encounter with Christ, his deep commitment was transferred to his new Lord.

The *fanatics,* on the other hand, are quite different from the fundamentalists. According to the dictionary, they are unreasonably enthusiastic people who are overly zealous. I think this definition is very tame. I believe that fanatics are not primarily driven by theology but by *an attitude of hate and self-righteousness*. They demonize whoever does not agree with them, and they tend to be legalistic and hypocritical. They are very similar to the Pharisees at the time of Jesus. I find fanatics to be the hardest Muslims to relate to. Some, but not all, fundamentalists are fanatical.

## JUSTICE AND GOD'S SOVEREIGNTY

Another assumption I have is that the *sovereignty of God can, and should, go hand in hand with our responsibility "to act justly and to love mercy and to walk humbly with [our] God"* (Micah 6:8). The sovereignty of God is one side of the coin, and our responsibility to act justly is the other side of the same coin. Jesus is the Prince of Peace, yet at the same time He said, "Blessed are the peacemakers" (Matthew 5:9). Abandoning either of the two sides of this coin could result in practicing injustice in the name of God or in living passive lives and washing our hands of any responsibility for action.

Recently, as I was reading the book of Genesis, I was struck by the contrast between Abraham and Jacob. Abraham had already been given by God the Promised Land, yet in Genesis 23 we see Abraham insisting on paying for the field where he wanted to bury his wife, Sarah. His confidence that God had given him the land did not release him from the responsibility to practice justice, nor did it give him the freedom to occupy land and take it by force. In contrast, we see in Genesis 27 how God promised the blessing to Jacob rather than to Esau, yet Jacob had a hard time trusting God to accomplish His purposes. So Jacob achieved what was promised to him through deception and lies rather than through trusting God and doing what was right. Did that please God?

## The Big War

One of the biggest assumptions I have is this: *Most Muslims are being pulled in one of two directions.* On the one hand, they are being pulled by *moderate, open-minded Muslims toward moderation and open-mindedness.* On the other hand, they are being pulled toward *fanatical Islam and/or toward Islamic fundamentalism.* My assumption here is that we, as Christians, and the governments of the United States, China, Europe, and other powerful countries around the world have a role to play in helping to *tip the scale* in the direction of moderation and open-mindedness by empowering the moderate Muslims.

The huge war that is waging today in our world is *for the souls and minds of Muslims.* John Mead, in his book *The New World War,* gives these definitions as he distinguishes three main types of Muslims:

- "*Cultural Muslims:* They adhere to social norms rather than to theology. In short, they are born into Islam.
- *Qur'anic Muslims:* They embrace the faith, and they adhere to the explicit teaching of the Qur'an. They follow Islam closely and seek, on a daily basis, to apply the teachings of the Qur'an to their lives. Some of these Qur'anic Muslims are fundamentalists.
- *Militant Muslims:* They actively engage in defending the faith by means of armed conflict and/or other strategic efforts aimed at the destruction or subjugation of non-Muslims who are understood to constitute a threat to the Islamic population in particular, or to the Islamic civilization in general."[2] This group includes some of the fundamentalists and all the militants and the fanatics.

Early in the twentieth century, the most powerful group in the Muslim world was the cultural Muslims. They were making a great impact on their countries by advocating modernity and secular education. In those days, Islam looked like the following diagram. In this right-side-up triangle, we see the minor role of the militants, or the fundamentalists. The perforated line allowed more and more militants to filter down to the second category, the Qur'anic Muslims. The second perforated line allowed more Qur'anic Muslims to filter down to the largest category, the powerful cultural Muslims.

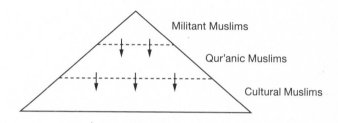

Nowadays the situation has changed dramatically. The triangle is no longer right side up. It is becoming more and more upside down. The moderates and open-minded Muslims are weak, and their voices are drowned out by the loud uproar of the fanatics, like some of those who preach in mosques on Fridays in Iraq and in other parts of the Muslim world. The legitimate but unaddressed grievances are making it relatively easy for militants to recruit support and volunteers to join their ranks. In this next diagram, the upside-down triangle, we see the situation of Islam in our world today.

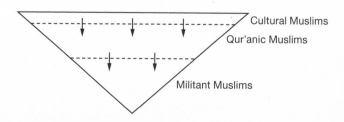

The perforated line on the top shows how the relatively small percentage of Muslims who are cultural Muslims are filtering through the perforated line and becoming Qur'anic Muslims. The second perforated line is allowing more and more Qur'anic Muslims to filter down and join the powerful militants. The success of *Hamas* in the elections of the Palestinian territories in February 2006 is but one illustration of this truth.

The war is waging for the souls and minds of the majority of Muslims who are being pulled in two directions. Should they move in the direction of moderate Islam and become open-minded? Or should they move in the direction of Islamic fundamentalism and fanaticism? The assumption I made earlier is this: *We, as Christians, and the governments of the United States, China, Europe, and other powerful nations have a role to play to help tip the scale in one of the two directions. Either we strengthen Islamic fundamentalism and fanaticism, or we strengthen moderate Muslims.* Furthermore, we as individuals have a role to play in whatever contacts we have with Muslims. *Either we draw the Muslims we know to open-mindedness and to Christ, or we push them away to fanaticism.* This diagram is another way of looking at this tug-of-war.

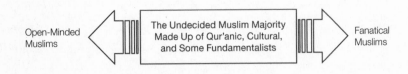

Open-Minded Muslims  |  The Undecided Muslim Majority Made Up of Qur'anic, Cultural, and Some Fundamentalists  |  Fanatical Muslims

As we attempt to unpack and address the issues that Ahmad raised, it is good to ask ourselves this question: How can I help Muslims I know or see move toward open-mindedness rather than fanaticism? Ultimately, our desire is for every Muslim we know to take a few steps closer to Christ.

## Two International Students

My older brother came to the United States in the 1950s as an international student. He came to study for his master's degree in engineering. Although my parents knew the Lord, they did not know how to articulate the gospel to us, so we grew up as nominal Christians who feared God. During his stay in the United States, my brother came to know Christ. The type of evangelicals that he connected with in America at that time attracted him to Jesus. When he went back to the Middle East, he started sharing the good news with us, and the gospel started penetrating our lives. Along with other people, God used my brother in my coming to know Christ.

*Sayyid Qutb*, on the other hand, was an Egyptian international student who came to America and had a very different experience. He was born in 1906, and as a boy, he memorized the whole of the Qur'an.* During his high school and college days, he drifted away from God and became a nominal or a cultural Muslim. However, he continued to enjoy the literary beauty of the Qur'an. He graduated from a teachers' college and became a teacher in Egyptian government schools. With time, the government recognized his sharp mind and in 1940 appointed him as an inspector of government schools. In the meantime, a very committed Egyptian Muslim, Hasan al-Banna, was leading the ever-growing organization known as the Muslim Brotherhood. Sayyid Qutb continued to be nominal in his faith, even though the Muslim Brotherhood was making a big impact on the lives of many Muslims in Egypt and the Middle East. In 1948, Sayyid Qutb was sent to Greeley, Colorado, with a unique scholarship. The Egyptian government, who gave him the scholarship, wanted him to return to Egypt and reform the educational system in his country. Furthermore, the Egyptian

---

* The Qur'an is almost as large as the New Testament.

government hoped that his exposure to America and to Americans would Westernize him. *While in America, he became a Muslim fundamentalist.* How did that happen?

To start with, he had never traveled outside his country. As he was on the ship heading to Europe and then to America, he panicked with this thought: If he could not live as a committed Muslim in Egypt, how could he survive as a Muslim in America? So he started reading the Qur'an, which he used to know by memory. The more he read and prayed, the more courage he had to approach other Egyptian Muslims on the ship. He gave them the same challenge that he faced, asking them how they could survive in London or in Paris if they could not live as victorious Muslims in Egypt. Then he invited them, one at a time, to his cabin to read the Qur'an together and to pray. One night, a beautiful drunk European woman barged into his cabin and made herself available to him. He was so scared that he closed the door in her face and knelt down to pray.

While in America, a few things attracted his critical eye. As I stated in a previous book, "He was impressed with the advanced technology, the efficient management, and the value of work and success, but he was very critical of the role of advertising and entertainment that in his view made America a lie." In Qutb's opinion, "The Americans' dedication to materialism, pragmatism and superficial religiosity made them a material body that had no soul or spirit. Their genius in industry and management was accompanied by primitiveness in spiritual and ethical values."[3] Qutb returned from America to Egypt a Muslim fundamentalist.

There were two events that took place during his stay in America that shook him to his core. He was amazed by the rejoicing of Americans about the assassination of Hasan al-Banna.* He wondered

---

\* Hasan al-Banna was the founder of the Muslim Brotherhood in Egypt and was perceived by people in the West to be the Osama bin Laden of his day.

how Americans could create caricatures of great men and make it justifiable to hate them. The other event that he witnessed was the enthusiasm of the West, and especially of the Christians, for the establishment of the state of Israel. He could not understand why Christians, who are supposed to promote justice, could forget all about justice when it came to siding with Israel.

When he returned to Egypt, he joined the Muslim Brotherhood and in time became one of its leaders. He wrote many books that were colored both by his experience in America and by his experience in the prisons of Egypt. He wrote *In the Shade of the Qur'an*, a complete commentary on the whole of the Qur'an. His most famous book, though, is *Milestones*, in which he summarized the philosophy and theology of Islamic fundamentalism. In 1966, he was hanged during the presidency of Jamal Abdul Nasser. At that time, the government in Egypt thought they had eradicated Islamic fundamentalism.

After reading so many books written by Muslims, I have come to the conclusion that *no one can eradicate Islamic fundamentalism*. We can root out a generation of fundamentalists, but if *legitimate grievances continue to be unaddressed*, a few years later, we will have to wage another war on a new generation of terrorists. What scares me is that every generation will be tougher to deal with because violence escalates. However, *we can marginalize the fanatics if we address the legitimate grievances* in the Middle East and thus strengthen the moderates in Islam and let *them* deal with the fanatics.

In 1966, the year that Qutb was hanged, Ayman al-Zawahri, then a teenager, was forming his first Muslims discipleship group. Zawahri became a disciple of Qutb by studying Qutb's books and becoming saturated with his theology. Ayman al-Zawahri is the number two man in Al Qaeda and is, in many ways, the brain of the movement. Muhammed Qutb, the brother of Sayyid Qutb, went to Saudi Arabia as a professor and taught at King Abdul Aziz University. One of the students, who was highly influenced by him, was Osama bin Laden.

My brother and Sayyid Qutb were *two international students who came to America*. My brother came to know Christ while in America, and he was the primary instrument in my coming to know Christ. Sayyid Qutb became an Islamic fundamentalist while in America and has had a major impact on Islamic fundamentalism today.

## QUESTIONS FOR REFLECTION AND DISCUSSION

1. Go back to the beginning of the chapter. What do you think of the statements made by Ahmad and by the Singaporean Christian?
2. What are some common assumptions you make about Islam and Muslims?
3. Consider your assumptions one at a time. How do they compare with
   a. the scriptural viewpoint?
   b. the worldview of Muslims?
4. Do you understand the various assumptions I made in this chapter? How do you feel about them?
5. How many personal contacts do you have among Muslims? Which Muslims do you pray for? How can you relate to them before you introduce them to Christ?

# CHAPTER 6

# THE CORE AND THE WRAPPINGS

*The evangelicals in America, under the leadership of the Religious Right, are trying to make America adhere to biblical values.*

— AN AMERICAN CHRISTIAN

In one of our conversations, Ahmad said to me, *"I get confused at times when American Christians talk to me about Christ. They give me the impression that for me to become a Christian, I need to believe in Christ and become a Rush Limbaugh fan."*\*

From 1991 to 2000, although I was living in Colorado, I continued to coach and visit my Egyptian friends and meet with them on a regular basis. For a period of two years we intentionally studied major themes

---

\*   Rush Limbaugh is a very conservative and famous radio talk show host in America.

in the Scriptures. We studied these themes through the entire Bible from Genesis to Revelation. One of the themes we studied was "What is the gospel, or the good news, to the Muslims?" Christ's message of good news to the people was "The kingdom of God is at hand." After spending many hours of study, I came to a simple definition of what that gospel is, and since then I fine-tuned my definition: The gospel is the *most fantastic* and great *news* that *people desperately need to* hear and know, not only on the cognitive level but experientially as well. It has to do with the facts that God is present with us despite all appearances, and God reigns and will triumph despite all appearances. These truths were revealed in *Jesus Christ* and in the *place of belongingness* that He offers.

## The Tangerine and the Wrappings

During the break just before our last session on the theme of the gospel, I went to my bedroom, wrapped a tangerine with a sheet of paper, and wrote on it, "I need to change my name from a Muslim name to a Christian name in order to enter the kingdom of God." Then I wrapped another paper around it and wrote on it, "I must stop using Muslim terminology such as *'Bismilaah Rahman Rahim'* ('In the name of God the Merciful the Compassionate') and start using Christian terminology like 'Hallelujah' and 'Praise the Lord.'" Then I wrapped it with another sheet and wrote on it, "I should become pro-Israel in my politics." This was followed by another sheet and another. By the time I finished, that tangerine was almost as big as a volleyball.

After the break, I joined the men for the concluding session on what the gospel (good news) is to the Muslims. I showed them that ball of paper and told them that inside it was something that symbolizes the gospel. I showed them what was written on the outside sheet and asked them, "Is this the gospel?" and they said, "No." Then

I peeled that outer sheet and showed them what was written and asked them the question, "Is this the gospel?" and they said, "No." I kept peeling, and the atmosphere of excitement was building up. When there was only one sheet left, they could tell there was a tangerine inside, and they started giggling. I asked them, "Is this the gospel?" and they yelled out, "No!" Then I peeled that last sheet off and held the tangerine in my hand and asked them, "Is this the gospel?" and they yelled out, "Yes!" But I said, "No." Then I peeled the tangerine and said, "This is the gospel!"

A few years ago I went to a physical therapist who was an atheist. His favorite bumper sticker was "God, save me from your followers." From the first session, when he found out that I am a Christian and work with The Navigators, a missionary organization, he started bashing the evangelicals and the Religious Right in America. I was tempted to defend, but then I reminded myself that the gospel is not our Western or our Christian wrappings, but the gospel is Jesus Christ and the place of belongingness that He offers. So I listened to him and agreed with him on a few things and apologized to him on behalf of my fellow Christians. Then I asked him the question, "How did Jesus offend you?" He was startled by my question and replied by saying, "Christ does not offend me at all." So we talked about the baby and the dirty bath water.

The story goes that a long time ago, a mother washed her baby in a small metal tub. When she was done, she picked up the baby, dried and dressed her, and put her in the crib. Since there was no indoor plumbing, the mother carried the small metal tub outside and emptied the dirty water. Of course she did not throw her baby out with the bath water! So I talked with the physical therapist about our need to differentiate between the bath water in our Christian history and the person of Jesus Christ.

In the many years I have known Muslims, I have come to believe that they are not offended by Christ but primarily by *our wrappings*. Gandhi, the great man of India, was very much attracted to Christ but not to our Christianity. His experience with Christians in England and in South Africa, before his final move to India, repulsed him. He was able, though, to differentiate between Christ and the dirty water. For many Muslims, it is hard to make that distinction.

What comes to the mind of a Muslim when he considers the possibility of believing in Christ and getting integrated into Christianity? What must he do to enter the kingdom of God? If I stand in his shoes, the following points might come to mind. How many of these ideas have to do with the gospel?[2]

- Change my name from a Muslim name like Ali to a Christian name like Steve.
- Believe that God had sex with Mary and that Jesus is their son.
- Get baptized right away and tell everyone about it, especially my family, or else Christians will be suspicious of my conversion.
- Give up kneeling like Muslims do when I pray. Pray while sitting on a chair or on a pew speaking to His Majesty. I should learn to relax and pray even with my legs crossed.
- Start attacking Islam, Muhammad, and the Qur'an to prove to myself and others that my total exodus from Islam is complete and therefore my belonging to Christianity is real. The more I attack Islam, the more Christians will truly believe that I have become one of them.
- If I am a woman, hang a golden cross around my neck, wear short skirts and sleeveless dresses, and stop wearing the hijab so I can show my Muslim family that I am no longer like them.
- Drink all the alcohol and eat all the pork that I want because I am free.

- Live without restraint and do anything I want because my sins are all forgiven.
- Be careful not to have slips of the tongue by using Muslim terminology such as "Al hamdulilaah" ("Thanks to God"), "Insha Allah" ("If God wills"), "Asalamu 'alaykum" ("Peace to you"), "Bismilaah" ("In the name of God"), and "Bismilaah Rahman Rahim" ("In the name of God the Merciful the Compassionate").
- See Arabs and Muslims as the enemy, calling their God a demon and their prophet Muhammad a terrorist and a demon-possessed pedophile.
- If I am living in the United States, become a Republican and listen to radio talk shows that support capitalism, democracy, Republicanism, and the Religious Right. I should attempt to become as Westernized as possible.

## OUR ATTITUDES

When our younger son was still a small child and we were living in Egypt, he needed to learn how to tie his shoelaces. In those days we did not have modern conveniences such as Velcro when it came to shoes. Every boy had to learn to tie his shoelaces. Our son at his young age found this to be challenging. One morning I wanted to take him to his school. When I went to his bedroom to call him, he was deeply absorbed in the challenging task of tying his shoelaces. I was so proud of him that I quietly called my wife, and we both stood by the door of his bedroom watching him. When he finally noticed us and saw my smile, he thought I was laughing at him, when in reality I was smiling because I was proud of him. So he started to weep and came at me and started hitting me. Do you think I hit him back? Of course not. I gave him a big hug and allowed him to continue to hit me *until his frustration melted in my love.*

In chapter 2 you got to see Ahmad's worldview. Did you find yourself arguing with him in your mind? As we unpack and address the issues that Ahmad raised, can we listen not only with our ears but also with our hearts? This process could result in our transformation. Ahmad represents over a billion Muslims in the world who need the good news of the gospel.

I used to think that the main truth in the book of Jonah had to do with the conversion of the Ninevites. The more I get into this book, however, the more I am coming to the conclusion that the book of Jonah is the story of a *missionary who needed to be converted.* I realize this sounds like an oxymoron, a missionary who needs conversion. I will get into the book of Jonah in more detail in a later chapter.

In Acts 10 we read the story of Cornelius and how God, through an angel, directed him to find answers to his yearnings. God could have easily given Cornelius the full message that he needed to hear through the angel. Instead, God wanted Peter to get involved and in the process become *transformed.* Peter could have ended up becoming an ethnocentric Jew if he hadn't gotten the exposure to the Gentiles that God desired for him.

Peter could not imagine himself entering the home of a Gentile. So God had to give him a vision and explain to him the meaning of the vision. The messengers arrived shortly after that and confirmed the vision and God's interpretation. So in obedience, Peter went to the home of Cornelius and took with him six Jewish Christian witnesses because he expected, upon his return, to be interrogated by the church in Jerusalem for entering the home of a Gentile. If Peter had not had the opportunity to see what God was doing among the Gentiles, perhaps the final conclusion by the Council in Jerusalem would have been different (see Acts 15). As Peter connected with Gentiles, not only were their lives changed, but he, too, was transformed in the process. While you read through this book, ask God to transform you.

Because Muslims need to hear the good news of the gospel, we might see ourselves as superior, since we are the bearers of the message and they are the recipients. We might be so preoccupied with their need that we miss out on what God wants to do in *our* lives. Like Jonah, we might be blind to our need for transformation.

In this chapter we looked at how the wrappings around the gospel are many times understood by Muslims to be a part of the essence of the gospel. We looked at how they tend to reject the message because of the wrappings we place around it. We also looked at what our attitude should be. It is not only the Muslims who need the message of the good news; we also need to be transformed in order to see Muslims through God's eyes.

## QUESTIONS FOR REFLECTION AND DISCUSSION

1. Go back to the beginning of the chapter. What do you think of the statements made by Ahmad and the American Christian?
2. Try to stand in the shoes of Muslims. What kinds of anxieties might they have about believing in Christ?
3. Take a look at the book of Jonah. What was the purpose of the book?
4. What kind of transformation do you need in order to have a healthy attitude toward Muslims?

# CHAPTER 7

# MILITANCY OR TOLERANCE

*The suicide bombing in London on July 7, 2005, was a form of barbarism. Suicide bombings do not make any sense, and it amazes me that these bombings do not get condemned by Muslims as they ought to be.*

— A British Christian

In his presentation of the Muslims' worldview, Ahmad said, *"When you read in your Bible how Samson died, do you perceive him as a terrorist? Do you blame Samson for using his only available weapon, his body, to kill innocent civilians?"*

Since 9/11, and over the years, I have received many e-mails and articles speaking of Islam as a religion of militancy. A *Washington Post–ABC News* poll on March 9, 2006, found that 46 percent of Americans have a negative view of Islam and Muslims, 7 percent higher than in the tense month after September 11, 2001. James J. Zogby, president of the Washington-based Arab American Institute, said he is not surprised by the poll's results. Politicians, authors, and media commentators in America have demonized the Arab world since 2001. He said, "The intensity has not abated and remains a vein that is very near the surface, ready to be tapped at any moment."[1]

In contrast, some people say that Islam means "peace," and therefore Islam is a religion of peace. The word *Islam* means "submission," and the word *salam* means "peace." The sound of the two words in Arabic is similar, because they come from the same root. In the midst of this confusion, some thoughtful friends wrote to me and wanted to know the truth. Is Islam a religion of tolerance or militancy? I believe that the Qur'an has both tolerance and militancy.

## CRITICAL DOCTRINES

There are three main Islamic doctrines, and the way they are interpreted will determine whether Muslims are cultural, Qur'anic, or militant. The three doctrines are *jihad, separation,* and *following the model of their prophet.*

*Jihad* is an Arabic word that means "striving." The first time I used the concordance of the Qur'an, I was looking for that word. I was surprised by the abundance of verses that mention the word *jihad*. There are three main interpretations for this doctrine.

1. Cultural Muslims believe that to practice jihad is to *strive to live a life of righteousness by avoiding sin.*

2. Qur'anic Muslims, on the other hand, believe that in order to practice jihad, it is not sufficient to strive to live a life of righteousness by avoiding sin. They go a step further by saying that *there should be social implications to that righteousness.* They call it in Arabic, *"Al amr bil ma'rouf wa nahy 'anil*

*munkar,*" which means *promoting virtue and preventing vice.*

3. Militant Muslims go even further in their interpretation of jihad. They say that *at times it is justifiable to use militancy to create the right environment so that Muslims can practice Islam properly.* If some people get killed in the process, it is considered collateral damage.

As for the doctrine of *separation*, I used to think there were only three interpretations for it, but since 9/11 I have discovered there is a fourth one.

1. Cultural and some Qur'anic Muslims believe that to be separate from the world means to *be in the world and yet not of the world.* In many ways this interpretation is also the interpretation many Christians have of what it means to be separate from the world.

2. Some Qur'anic Muslims go further by believing that the true interpretation of separation is to *relate and have fellowship only with like-minded committed Muslims.* So a committed Muslim living in Cairo, Egypt, should be motivated by duty and by commitment to drive five kilometers from his apartment to do his shopping at a supermarket owned by a committed Muslim like himself. He should not be lazy by doing his shopping at the nearby supermarket owned by a cultural Muslim.

3. Some Qur'anic Muslims and some fundamentalists go even further in their understanding of separation from the world. They believe that separation does not occur unless *committed people live together in communes.* The Amish in America practice that understanding of separation. The biggest experiment with this theology in the recent history of Islam took place with the Taliban in Afghanistan.

4. A very small segment of militant Muslims go much further in interpreting this doctrine in a unique way. Trusted, committed Muslims who belong to the "house of Islam" can be sent out to the "house of war," or the enemy land, to live there as *sleepers*. The duty of the sleeper is to appear to be fully assimilated so that he can fulfill the mission for which he was sent. Some Muslim fundamentalists who are sleepers might force themselves to sin and drink alcohol a few days before the mission begins in order to deceive whoever is watching them. They might want to create the image that they are beyond suspicion.

The third doctrine has to do with what it means to *follow in the footsteps of their prophet Muhammad* on a daily basis. For this doctrine there are three main interpretations.

1. There are some folk Muslims, Qur'anic Muslims, and Muslim fundamentalists who will try to imitate their prophet Muhammad in his behavior to the point that they *regress to a seventh-century mentality*. Most Muslims around the world do not agree with this interpretation of what it means to follow in the footsteps of Muhammad and are embarrassed by those who believe in it. Many of the men who wear white robes and sandals and grow beards are not imitating their prophet by regressing to the seventh century, however. The same is true of many women who cover their heads and in some cases their faces except for the eyes. These people are simply making a statement that they refuse to assimilate into modernity and all the evils that come with it.

2. Many Muslims who are moderate in their practice of Islam believe that to follow in the footsteps of their prophet Muhammad is to *identify evil as he did and have the courage to confront it*. Muhammad dared to confront the evil of

worshiping idols and risked his life for it. Many gods were worshiped in the city of Mecca, and four months of the year were dedicated to the pilgrimage. Pilgrims came to the city, and the businesses thrived during those four months. Muhammad's message centered on the fact that there is only one God, and His name is Allah.* Muhammad's focus on the oneness of God and his claim that all other gods are idols was a blunt confrontation to the idol worship that flourished in Mecca. Because of this, he was hated and persecuted to the degree that he, along with his followers, had to flee from the city of Mecca and move to the city of Medina in 622. Furthermore, Muhammad identified other forms of evil that were practiced by the Arabs in the city of Mecca at that time, and he confronted those evils as well. Muslims who adhere to this interpretation believe that they should *identify the evil of our day and have the courage to confront it.*

3. Muslim fundamentalists have a powerful interpretation of this doctrine. They look at the life of their prophet Muhammad as he went through three main stages — *underground, consolidation and discipleship*, and finally *expansion* — and believe that they should follow similar steps. If they get imprisoned, they see themselves like their prophet in the *underground stage* when he was persecuted in Mecca.

---

* Allah is the Arabic word for God. When I pray in Arabic, I pray to Allah. He is the Father of the Lord Jesus Christ. The Arabic Bible is full of this word. We do not have another word for God in Arabic. Does that mean the God the Muslims worship is the same as our God? The answer is yes and no. Muslims believe that God has ninty-nine names or attributes. Christians agree with most of these attributes. One major difference, though, is that they do not believe that God is our heavenly Father. Another way of looking at it is by asking this question: Was the Yahweh that Jesus talked about the same Yahweh that the Pharisees talked about? The answer is yes and no. The similarities are obvious, but when Jesus taught His disciples to pray, He told them to address God as Father. The Pharisees must have been shocked by this teaching and must have considered it a heresy.

Once they get released from prison, they see this as following in Muhammad's footsteps as he moved with his followers to Medina. This was the beginning of the *consolidation and discipleship stage*. Muhammad consolidated his followers in Medina, and for the first time, Muslims were able to worship God in freedom. This second stage led to the inevitable stage of *expansion within their cities and other cities, tribes, and countries*.

I have read many books written by twentieth-century Muslim fundamentalists and have learned a great deal about how they live their lives even while in prison. Some Muslim fundamentalists who are arrested and imprisoned become more deeply committed to Islamic fundamentalism during their imprisonment. While in prison they do not have to wake up at sunrise, but they choose to do that because they want to pray the sunrise prayer together. They spend the whole day studying the Qur'an, memorizing it, discussing issues in small groups, and listening to their leaders teach and preach. When the time for their release from prison comes, they see it as graduation day from "seminary," and from day one they start "the ministry." So a Muslim fundamentalist can know exactly which stage he is in, whether the underground stage, the consolidation and discipleship stage, or the expansion stage. There is *a meaning and a purpose to life at every stage*. For them, there is no room for self-pity or for having a victim mentality.

## The Qur'an on Tolerance and Militancy

There are several passages in the Qur'an that talk about tolerance. The most quoted passage teaches, "There should be no compulsion in religion" (Surah 2:256). In other words, Islam should not be forced on any non-Muslims. Non-Muslims are free to worship God the way they choose. Another passage states, "If your Lord had so wished, everyone on earth would have believed, all of them together! So will you force mankind to become believers?" (Surah 10:99). And a further passage that shows tolerance in the Qur'an is Surah 18:29: "SAY: 'Truth comes from your Lord. Let anyone who wishes to, believe, and let anyone who wishes to, disbelieve.'"

Still another powerful passage is Surah 42:48: "If they should still evade it, We did not send you [Muhammad] as any guardian over them; you have only to state things plainly." This last passage points out clearly that Muhammad's job was not to play the role of the keeper or guardian, preventing people from leaving Islam. Fanatical Muslims tend to either consciously or unconsciously skip over verses like these.

Then there are passages in the Qur'an that talk about intolerance and militancy. Fundamentalists focus on the militant passages, while moderate and liberal Muslims focus on the tolerant passages. It is interesting, though, that one particular key passage is used by both liberals and fundamentalists in their arguments. The text is Surah 2:190-193, which says,

> Fight those who fight against you along God's way, yet do not initiate hostilities; God does not love aggressors. Kill them wherever you may catch them, and expel them from anywhere they may have expelled you. Sedition [*Fitna*] is more serious than killing! Yet do not fight them at the Hallowed Mosque unless they fight you there. If they should fight you, then fight them back; such is the reward for disbelievers. However if they stop, God will be Forgiving, Merciful. Fight them until there is no more subversion and [all] religion belongs to God. If they stop, let there be no [more] hostility except towards wrongdoers.

The tolerants' interpretation of this text states that Muslims are not to initiate conflicts, and as soon as direct hostilities end, peace is to be sought at all cost. They focus on these phrases in this text: "Do not initiate hostilities; God does not love aggressors. . . . Do not fight them . . . unless they fight you." Fighting is allowed only in self-defense.

The fundamentalists' interpretation, based on the same text, concludes that Muslims must fight all non-Muslims until Islam dominates the world and infidels are brought under submission. They focus on these phrases in this text: "Fight those who fight against you along God's way. . . . Kill them wherever you may catch them, and expel them from anywhere they may have expelled you. . . . Fight them back; such is the reward for disbelievers. . . . Fight them until there is . . . no [more] hostility except towards wrongdoers."

## THE MODERATES' ARGUMENT

The argument of the moderate Muslims is based on the assumption that certain parts of the Qur'an were relevant only at the time of Muhammad. Other parts of the Qur'an, they believe, have a universal application, not only at the time of Muhammad but throughout history. The great example of this theory was proposed by Mahmoud Taha, a Sudanese theologian who was hanged in 1985 in Sudan because of his theology. In his book *The Second Message of Islam*, he presented his theory in detail. Mahmoud Taha believed that Muhammad was given a supreme revelation in the early years when he was in Mecca.*

According to Taha, because Muhammad's message was pure and

---

\* Meccan Surahs presented Muhammad as a warner to draw his people out of idolatry. The Surahs were prophetic and exhortative. They were short. The main themes of this period had to do with God's oneness, the Day of Judgment, God's goodness and power, man's response of gratitude to God, and worship and care for the poor. Pride in wealth was considered ingratitude to God and a denial of the Creator.

the people were not ready for it, he was harassed and persecuted. He and his followers considered running for their lives to Ethiopia. Later on they decided that it would be more strategic if they fled to the city of Medina, which they did in 622. The city of Medina was about 250 miles north of Mecca in Saudi Arabia.

Mahmoud Taha wrote that in Medina, Muhammad was given a diluted message to give to the people because they were not ready for the supreme message due to the hardness of their hearts.* The way Taha perceived the supreme message was equivalent to the way we perceive the Sermon on the Mount. Taha believed that Muslims should go back to the supreme message, the revelation that was given to Muhammad in Mecca. He and his followers believed that the Meccan Surahs should be given more weight over the message that was given to Muhammad in Medina. The supreme message focused on God and His attributes, on tolerance, and on caring for widows and orphans, while the diluted message that was given later during the Medina stage included intolerance and militancy.

Dr. A. A. An-Na'im, a liberal Muslim and a legal scholar and human-rights activist, is one of Mahmoud Taha's disciples. He received law degrees from Sudan and Cambridge University and a PhD in law from the University of Edinburgh in Scotland. He has focused on how much Taha's interpretation of Islam is compatible with Western notions of human rights. He said,

> Unless the basis of modern Islamic law is shifted away from those texts of the Qur'an and Sunna of the Medina stage, which constituted the foundations of the constructions of

---

* In the Medina Surahs in the Qur'an, Muhammad is presented as the leader of the community. He is Rasoul Allah, the Messenger of God. The Surahs are long, and they deal with the details of the law similar to the book of Leviticus. They address the waywardness of people and the judgment to come. Militancy and intolerance appear in this part of the Qur'an.

Shari'a, there is no way of avoiding drastic and serious violation of universal standards of human rights. . . . As stated and
explained in relation to constitutionalism, criminal justice,
and international law, the traditional techniques of reform
within the framework of Shari'a are inadequate for achiev-
ing the necessary degree of reform. To achieve that degree of
reform, we must be able to set aside clear and definite texts of
the Qur'an and Sunna of the Medina stage as having served
their transitional purpose and implement those texts of the
Meccan stage which were progressively inappropriate for the
practical application but are now the only way to proceed.[2]

Mahmoud Taha and An-Na'im are perceived by most Muslims
to be very liberal, and yet they are still considered Muslims. The book
*Liberal Islam* did not exclude them as heretics but included them among
liberal Muslims, even though Kurzman, the editor, does not agree with
their theology.

## THE FUNDAMENTALISTS' ARGUMENT

To discuss the fundamentalists' argument, we need to address the theory
of abrogation. Abrogation means that later revelation has more weight
than earlier revelation. Abrogation came into existence in Islam after
the incident of the Satanic Verses. To understand the issues of abrogation and the Satanic Verses, we need to cover very briefly some history.

According to Muslim historians, Muhammad had a supernatural
experience in 610 during his time with God. Because of his marriage to
Khadijah, the rich widow, Muhammad had the luxury of being able to
spend hours in prayer. He was gripped with a burning issue: Why did
God forsake the Arabs? The Jews had their own prophets and their own
book in their own language. The Christians had their own prophet

(he thought Jesus was the prophet to the Christians) and their own book in their own language.* How come the Arabs had no prophet of their own and no book of their own in their own language? As Muhammad was in prayer before God struggling with this burning issue, Muslims believe that the angel Gabriel appeared to him in another supernatural experience. That experience in 612 gave Muhammad the assurance of his call to prophethood. (Muslims believe that from 610 to 632, the date of his death, Muhammad received revelation, a few sentences at a time, from God alongside his thoughts.)

This revelation that came to him through the angel Gabriel was, according to Muslims, from the Book that is in heaven (*Al Lawh al Mahfouz*). Muslims believe that parts of that Book were given to Moses (*Tawrat*), and other parts were given to David (*Zabour*). Those parts combined to form the Old Testament. Other parts were given to Jesus, who in turn gave to His disciples (*Injil*), and they formed the New Testament. Muhammad differed from all those who came before him because he was illiterate. Moses, David, and Jesus knew how to read and write, but Muhammad did not. Therefore, the revelation that he received was dictated to him word by word, a few sentences at a time. He memorized what he received and quickly dictated it to someone who knew how to read and write. Muslims believe that the Qur'an has the actual words from the Book in heaven. The contents of the Qur'an are, in a sense, a photocopy of the words in the Book that is in heaven. What Christians believe about the Ten Commandments, Muslims believe about the whole of the Qur'an.

Now back to the incident of the Satanic Verses. Muhammad's message to the Meccans centered on the belief that the gods the Meccans were worshiping were mere idols and that there is only one true God. This message was met by great resistance from the businessmen in Mecca who profited from the business generated by the four months

---

* Syriac language, an ancient language that existed at that time.

of pilgrimage. So Muhammad and his followers were harassed and persecuted. Many people in Mecca worshiped three goddesses named *Allaat, Uzzah,* and *Manaat.* Muhammad wondered if they could be worshiped along with the one God without contradicting His oneness. As he thought of Christianity, he saw no contradiction between believing in God and at the same time believing in the existence of angels. So that day he believed he received a revelation from God that it was acceptable to believe in Him as well as believing in the three goddesses. That made the people in Mecca very happy, and they became more open to Muhammad's message.

Very soon Muhammad realized that this was a huge mistake and believed that Satan had slipped this wrong theological thought into his mind as he was receiving revelation. This is what is known as the Satanic Verses (see Surah 53:19-23). Muslims believe that another revelation came to Muhammad at a later time that corrected the Satanic Verses. The theory of abrogation is based on that event. That theory states, *Later revelation has more weight than previous revelation.* When he was asked whether God can change His mind by giving contradictory revelations, Muhammad responded that God is the absolute Sovereign of the universe, and He can alter His commands. The Qur'an says, "We do not cancel any verse nor let it be forgotten; instead We bring something better than it or else something similar. Do you not know that God is Capable of everything?" (Surah 2:106). This became the foundation of the theory of abrogation.

According to an early verse (Surah 2:219), drinking wine can have good and bad effects. But according to a later text (Surah 5:93-94), alcohol is abolished altogether. The later revelation abrogates, or cancels out, the previous revelation. In Mecca, the disciples were encouraged to pray and recite the Qur'an all night (see Surah 73:2-4). In Medina, the daily concerns increased, so Muhammad received a revelation that Muslims did not need to pray all night; the command was relaxed (see Surah 73:20).

These illustrations about alcohol and prayer at night are harmless.

When it comes to tolerance and militancy, though, the issue takes on utmost importance. In the order of chronological revelation, tolerance precedes militancy. So when the abrogation principle is applied, texts in the Qur'an that address the issue of militancy have more weight than texts that deal with tolerance, since they were revealed at a later time. Muslim fundamentalists and militants take the theory of abrogation very seriously and believe they have a stronger theological case than moderate and liberal Muslims.

In contrast to the fundamentalists, Mahmoud Taha and his disciple An-Nai'm reversed abrogation because they believed that the early supreme revelation has more weight than the later revelation that addressed a certain historical context of that time and *served a transitional purpose.*

Is there something similar to the theory of abrogation in the Bible? We do have something similar. In 1 Samuel 15:1-3, we see this text:

> Samuel said to Saul, "I am the one the LORD sent to anoint you king over his people Israel; so listen now to the message from the LORD. This is what the LORD Almighty says: 'I will punish the Amalekites for what they did to Israel when they waylaid them as they came up from Egypt. Now go, attack the Amalekites and totally destroy everything that belongs to them. Do not spare them; *put to death men and women, children and infants,* cattle and sheep, camels and donkeys.'" (emphasis added)

And in Deuteronomy 7:1-2, Moses taught the people of God to do the following:

> When the LORD your God brings you into the land you are entering to possess and drives out before you many nations — the Hittites, Girgashites, Amorites, Canaanites,

Perizzites, Hivites and Jebusites, seven nations larger and stronger than you—and when the LORD your God has delivered them over to you and you have defeated them, *then you must destroy them totally. Make no treaty with them, and show them no mercy.* (emphasis added)

By todays standards, what Samuel wanted King Saul to do and what Moses taught the people to do is perceived as *ethnic cleansing.* Yet when we look at the New Testament, we see a different teaching. In Matthew 5:43-48 we see Jesus teaching His disciples:

You have heard that it was said, "Love your neighbor and hate your enemy." But I tell you: *Love your enemies and pray for those who persecute you, that you may be sons of your Father in heaven.* He causes his sun to rise on the evil and the good, and sends rain on the righteous and the unrighteous. *If you love those who love you, what reward will you get?* Are not even the tax collectors doing that? And if you greet only your brothers, what are you doing more than others? Do not even pagans do that? *Be perfect, therefore, as your heavenly Father is perfect.* (emphasis added)

To which of the two teachings do we give more weight, the Old Testament texts or what Jesus taught about how we should treat even our enemies? In our case, the New Testament came later in time than the Old Testament. But in the Qur'an, this teaching about tolerance and militancy is reversed, so Muslim fundamentalists, who take the theory of abrogation seriously, have a strong theological case within Islam.

## SUICIDE BOMBINGS

We hear so much about suicide bombings, and we are shocked and bewildered and wonder, *How could people do that?* But are we shocked by what Samson did when he used his only available weapon—his body—to kill innocent civilians? The way we see Samson is the way Muslims see suicide bombers. Is committing suicide in battle a new phenomenon?

During World War II, Japanese airplane pilots committed suicide in their strategic missions and were highly respected by the Japanese people. Some American pilots, after reaching strategic positions in their last flight, decided to cross the *line of no return** and were willing to give their lives for bringing the war to an end. These pilots were models of courage, patriotism, and self-sacrifice.

How did suicide bombing become a popular tool used by the Palestinians, Iraqis, and others in recent history?

1. During the Iraq and Iran war in the eighties, Iranian teenage boys volunteered to serve in the army. They were too young, and there was not enough time to train them. So they volunteered to walk in long lines in front of the army and step on land mines planted by the Iraqis. They were highly respected.

2. Hezbollah members in Lebanon are highly respected by the Lebanese for their social work. They are very involved in providing services at extremely low costs to the poor, who could otherwise not afford to pay for the essential services. Hezbollah members are also involved in resisting, through military means, the Israeli presence in south Lebanon because they perceive Sheb'a farms as Lebanese land taken

---

* The "line of no return" refers to the line in the gas indicator in the cockpit of a fighter airplane showing that the gas tank is half full and that the pilot has just enough gas to take him back to safety.

by Israel. They are also very much involved in the political process in Lebanon. For years Hezbollah has had strong links with Iran since they are both Shi'ites. The *idea of suicide bombing transitioned from Iran to Hezbollah* in Lebanon.

3. In December 1992, Israelis blindfolded and shackled 415 Palestinians and deported them to the belt in south Lebanon that Israel created. Many of them were Hamas leaders who were doctors, professors, businessmen, and some prisoners. They were left in that very cold month of December without food, blankets, and tents. The Lebanese government did nothing to help them. In addition to two prominent Christians, the people who cared for them during that tough time were men from Hezbollah who dared to reach out to them with much-needed supplies.* They ended up spending prolonged time with these Palestinians and *passed to them what they learned from the Iranians about the idea of suicide bombing.*

4. Some Palestinians, including Hamas, started using this method of resistance to fight against the Israeli occupation, and the mass media facilitated its spread to Iraq, Russia, and other parts of the world.

People in the West look down on suicide bombing as a savage way of practicing terrorism, and *I agree with this assessment. I wish these Palestinians practiced nonviolent resistance.* Suicide bombing practiced by the Palestinians is an expression of their hopelessness. Palestinians would be *infinitely more effective* if nonviolence were evident in their actions and rhetoric.

On the other hand, Muslims see the suicide bombers as models,

---

* The two prominent Christians were Leonard Rodgers and Brother Andrew. As a result of Brother Andrew's visits, he made valuable connections with Hamas leaders that continued over the years. Some of the chapters in his book *Light Force* give an account of his experiences with Hamas.

courageous men and women who are willing to lay down their lives to resist the oppressors. When Palestinians threw stones at armored vehicles as they faced an army made up of tanks, guns, and airplanes, it looked weak. So the Palestinians improvised a new weapon, basically their bodies, in order to have more of a "fair chance" in this "unfair battle." Some volunteered to become suicide bombers for what they perceive as noble purposes; others did for primitive motivations, such as a quick escape from miserable living into heaven, with all its waiting pleasures.

In a letter I wrote to President Bush in April 2002, I included a paragraph about suicide bombers. I personally believe that if Palestinians and other oppressed people in the world followed in the footsteps of Gandhi, Martin Luther King Jr., and ultimately Jesus Christ by practicing nonviolent resistance, our world would be a different place today. Here is a paragraph from my letter to the president:

> The mass media in the States is trying to present the suicide bombers as greedy murderers going after money for their families promised by Saddam Hussein or others. From what I studied about Islamic fundamentalism, this is not a correct interpretation. In the West Bank and Gaza, these suicide bombers are perceived as courageous people who are willing to die for freedom. They are desperate people in a very desperate situation with no hope for the future. I personally think that these suicide bombers start with "temporary insanity," but with prolonged life under daily oppression, their temporary insanity changes in their minds to reasonable patriotism.

In this chapter we looked at a number of doctrines and beliefs. We learned how each of them has several interpretations. The kind of interpretation a Muslim believes will determine whether he or she will become a moderate or a fundamentalist. It will also determine whether or not that person is open to considering the Christian faith.

## QUESTIONS FOR REFLECTION AND DISCUSSION

1. Reread the epigraph by the British Christian at the beginning of the chapter. What do you think of this statement and of Ahmad's statements about suicide bombings?
2. What similarities do you observe between jihad in Islam and armed struggle in other religions? For example, in 1995 right-wing Israeli radical Yigal Amir assassinated Israel's prime minister, Yitzhak Rabin, because he disagreed with the Oslo Peace Accords. How does this equate to the rage of the jihadis?
3. Do the fundamentalists' interpretations of separation and following in the footsteps of Muhammad seem reasonable?
4. What do you think of the theory of abrogation? What makes it dangerous in Islam?
5. Why do you think young men and women are willing to commit suicide for their Muslim faith? If you stand in their shoes, can you understand their motivations?

PART TWO

# THE MESSAGE

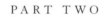

UNPACKING THE
ISSUES

# CHAPTER 8

# LIVING AMONG
# THE NATIONS

*If they want to access our pure theology, they will need
to learn our Christian vocabulary.*

— A JORDANIAN CHRISTIAN

*The Bible teaches that we need to be separate from the
world.*

— AN UZBEK CHRISTIAN

When he presented the Muslims' worldview to me,
Ahmad said, *"Since you are so eager for us to understand your religion, why don't you use a language we
can understand?"* Ahmad also told me, *"There were
some Christians in Egypt who connected well with us
Muslims, but it seemed to me that the majority preferred
to be isolated from us. I have often wondered whether
the Bible teaches isolationism."*

In this chapter I want to draw your attention to two great periods in the history of the Old Testament regarding the people of God. These are the periods of their captivity in Egypt and their exile in Babylon. Both have much to teach us regarding our relationships with Muslims today. But first, there are a couple of matters we need to discuss: the issue of ethnocentricity versus being a blessing, and what I call "the three pictures."

A Christian domestic helper from Southeast Asia came to work at the home of a Muslim family in North Africa. The ability of this woman to speak English was extremely limited. Furthermore, the family, made up of a father, mother, and six-year-old girl, also spoke very little English. However, the only way for this domestic helper and the Muslim family to communicate with each other was through the international language of English. The domestic helper loved the Lord. Her humility, love, and selfless service were a very attractive testimony to Christ. She loved this family and became like a second mother to the six-year-old girl, in spite of the limited communication abilities on both sides.

One day the little girl barged into the room of the domestic helper and found her on her knees praying. The girl politely waited until the domestic helper finished and then, in her limited English, asked her, "Were you praying?" The answer was, "Yes." "Who do you speak to when you pray?" the girl asked. "To Christ," the domestic helper responded. The girl asked, "Will you please teach me how to pray to Christ?" The domestic helper said, "I do not know how to pray in English, only Tagalog, my native language."*

The girl pleaded to the domestic helper to teach her how to pray, even if it had to be in Tagalog! At her insistence, the domestic helper dictated a prayer in Tagalog, and the girl wrote down the words in Arabic letters without understanding the meaning of the words. Shortly

---

* Tagalog is one of the languages in the Philippines.

afterward, the domestic helper left the family and returned to her country. The girl continued for the next decade to pray to Christ every night before she went to sleep, in a language she did not understand.

One night when she was a teenager, she was in her room listening to her small short-wave radio. All of a sudden she heard someone speaking in Arabic, and she recognized that the name *Masih,* or Christ, was mentioned frequently by the speaker. For years she had addressed her prayer every night to Christ. Most of what she was hearing on the radio, though, she could not understand. True, the message she heard was in Arabic, and Arabic was her language, yet the words were strange and unfamiliar. The great news for her came at the end of the program. The speaker said, "Tomorrow, and every night at the same time, there will be a continuation of this program."

*Finally God has answered my prayer,* she thought. That night she did not dare to touch the tuner on the radio out of fear that she might not be able to find the station the next day since it was a short-wave station. From that night on, she listened to the Christian station for fifteen minutes every night. It took her about six months of listening before she realized that the word *Yasou',* the Christian Arabic word for Jesus, which the speaker frequently referred to, meant the same as the word *Isa,* which is the Arabic word for Jesus in the Qur'an.*

As God was watching this young lady yearning to know His beloved Son, how do you suppose He felt about His Arab church reaching out to the people of the Middle East through that radio program? How do you think God feels about the manner in which we reach out to people around us? Are we making a serious effort to share the gospel with them in a language they are familiar with and can easily comprehend?

---

* Yasou' is the Arabic word that Arab Christians use for Jesus, and it is close to the Hebrew name for Jesus (Yashou'). Isa, the Arabic word for Jesus in the Qur'an, is closer to the Greek name for Jesus. Yashou' in Hebrew and Yisus in Greek are names for the same person. Both Muslims and Christian Arabs use the same word for Christ.

My point in telling this story is that Arab Christians over the centuries have persisted in using a Christian religious language, which is strange and unfamiliar to Arab Muslims. In many parts of the world, we Christians tend to erect barriers through our ethnocentricity, rather than trying to build bridges.

## ETHNOCENTRICITY VERSUS BEING A BLESSING

Ethnocentricity offers a place of belongingness at the cost of exclusion. We belong to different races, nations, cultures, and subcultures. People who belong to subcultures tend to have their own distinct languages, customs, and values. No wonder the young North African girl in our story could not understand more than 30 percent of what was being broadcast on the Christian program, even though it was in Arabic! Many Arab Christians in the Middle East have their own distinct subculture and religious language, and they tend to intermarry and live an isolated lifestyle among Muslims.

Throughout their history, the Jews needed to relate to other people groups and live their lives, as it were, on a "balance beam." The people of God in Old Testament times needed to be *separate from the nations* around them so they would not get contaminated by their idolatry. This was a big danger to those who stayed behind in the land during the Exile and, to some degree, to some of those who returned from the Exile.

Yet they also needed to be a *blessing to the nations*. Abraham, the great patriarch, was told by God, "Leave your country . . . and go to the land I will show you. I will make you into a great nation and I will bless you . . . and all peoples on earth will be blessed through you" (Genesis 12:1-3). The way Abraham related to the nations of his day was quite different from the way Joshua or Samuel related to their neighbor nations. The Jews were given a *privilege* and a *responsibility*.

It was easy for them to hold tight to the *privilege*, but many times they forgot about the *responsibility*.

This was a temptation not only for the people of God in Old Testament times. It has been a temptation for the people of God through all the ages and everywhere around the world. It is very easy to become ethnocentric.

On the night before His crucifixion, Jesus poured out His heart to God the Father, praying for His disciples and for us, too (see John 17:20). He was deeply concerned that His disciples would stay and live, as it were, on the balance beam. He did not want them to be so separated from the world that they became an alienated ethnocentric community or so much in the world that they became worldly.

Jesus did not want His followers to lose their "saltiness" and become useless (Matthew 5:13). In His prayer Jesus said,

> "I am coming to you now, but I say these things while I am still in the world. . . . I have given them your word and the world has hated them, for they are not of the world any more than I am of the world. My prayer is not that you take them out of the world but that you protect them from the evil one. They are not of the world, even as I am not of it. Sanctify them by the truth; your word is truth. As you sent me into the world, I have sent them into the world." (John 17:13-18)

His prayer is loaded with descriptions of what it is like to stay and live on the balance beam. Christians are not *of* the world, yet they are *in* the world, and they are supposed to be salt and light. Jesus said to His disciples,

> "You are the salt of the earth. . . . You are the light of the world. A city on a hill cannot be hidden. Neither do people light a

lamp and put it under a bowl. Instead they put it on its stand, and it gives light to everyone in the house. In the same way, let your light shine before men, that they may see your good deeds and praise your Father in heaven." (Matthew 5:13-16)

## THE THREE PICTURES

As I thought of God's people in the world, three mental pictures came to mind. Here is picture 1:

In this first picture I have drawn those who are born-again as only partially affected by the gospel. I filled their heads only. They are a "holy huddle." They are separated from the mainstream of society because of their fears, insecurities, and Christian subculture. They do not know how to relate to the unchurched, and they cover their insecurity by appearing to be very holy. They are afraid of getting contaminated by the world, so they separate themselves from the world. Jonah was very much an example of a picture 1 kind of missionary. He himself was ethnocentric and was representative of the people of God, who were ethnocentric at that time.

In picture 2 we have the other extreme:

Here we see another group of born-again Christians who are partially affected by the gospel. Thus, as with the first group, I filled only their heads and not their whole bodies. These Christians differ radically from the born-again Christians in picture 1, yet they are equally misguided. In picture 2, the Christians are very much *in the world, but they have become worldly.* They are messengers who have lost their message. When they muster the courage to connect with people in the mainstream, the response they get is, "Who are you to tell me about Christ? I do not see anything in your life that makes you a credible witness to Christ."

Queen Esther in the Old Testament was tempted to be a picture 2 person when she became one of King Xerxes' wives. She was afraid to approach the king, her husband, and ask for a favor regarding her people. Esther was motivated by fear and by her desire to maintain her comfort zone. Her Jewish relative and mentor, Mordecai, sent her the challenging message that if she was not willing to risk her life to save God's people, then God would use someone else and would place her "on the shelf." So she composed herself and moved back to the balance beam, which is represented in picture 3:

In picture 3, note that I filled the whole bodies of the people, not just their heads. The gospel is influencing their total lives, and they are being transformed as they live in the world. They are in the midst of the mainstream of human life. *They are in the world, and yet they are not of the world.* They are on the balance beam trying not to fall either toward picture 1 or picture 2. They are salt and light. They are good yeast permeating their society with grace and truth.

A shocking picture of *separation from the world* appears in Paul's first letter to the Corinthians. Paul wrote to the church challenging the leadership to take firm action against one of the church members who was having a sexual relationship with his stepmother.* Paul wrote,

> I have written you in my letter not to associate with sexually immoral people — not at all meaning the people of this world who are immoral, or the greedy and swindlers, or idolaters. In that case you would have to leave this world. But now I am writing you that you must not associate with anyone who calls himself a brother but is sexually immoral or greedy, an idolater or a slanderer, a drunkard or a swindler. With such a man do not even eat. (5:9-11)

It is interesting that the separation in this text is not from the immoral people who are in the world. If Christians separate themselves from those in the world, they will become like picture 1. If, on the other hand, they compromise by allowing the unrepentant sinner to continue to live in sin, they are being like picture 2. Paul challenged them to separate themselves not from the non-Christians but from the born-again Christians who were sexually immoral, greedy, or idolaters.

What is Paul's message to me in this text? Could it be that I should not separate myself from Muslims and the unchurched in order to not end up like picture 1? These are the people God has called me to live among as salt and light. Could it be that the people I should separate myself from are the born-again Christians who hate Muslims, demonize them, and live with self-righteousness and a superior attitude toward the unchurched? Could it be that if I stayed around these judgmental

---

\* I am assuming that this church member was a born-again Christian.

Christians I might become snobbish and exclusive and motivated by ethnocentricity rather than by love? If this is the right interpretation, then this is very radical teaching. It is quite radical to love Muslims and avoid arrogant born-again Christians.

## THE CAPTIVITY IN EGYPT

We all know about Jacob's dysfunctional family in which Joseph grew up. We know how Joseph ended up in Egypt after his brothers betrayed him. We also know how he found himself in a prison in Egypt as a result of Potiphar's wife's hurt pride. God in His grace gave Pharaoh, the king of one of the superpowers of the day, a dream. In this dream He informed Pharaoh about the future economy over the next fourteen years. Can you imagine the president of the United States getting information from God about the best investments in the next seven years and how the economy will go during the next fourteen years?

Pharaoh could not understand the symbols of the dream, so God in His grace gave Joseph the ability to interpret dreams. By this means the connection between Joseph and the pharaoh was established. Joseph was appointed as the ruler, or the prime minister, of Egypt and was given responsibility for planning the economy. He had quite an advantage in knowing what to do, since he understood that God had revealed to the pharaoh in the dream that there would be seven years of abundance followed by seven years of starvation. *How did Joseph plan for the future, and what were the consequences?*

In Genesis 46 we have a record of how Joseph tried to address the situation:

> Then Joseph said to his brothers and to his father's household, "I will go up and speak to Pharaoh and will say to him, 'My brothers and my father's household, who were living in the

land of Canaan, have come to me. The men are shepherds; they tend livestock, and they have brought along their flocks and herds and everything they own.' When Pharaoh calls you in and asks, 'What is your occupation?' you should answer, 'Your servants have tended livestock from our boyhood on, just as our fathers did.' Then you will be allowed to settle in the region of Goshen, for all shepherds are detestable to the Egyptians." (verses 31-34)

There is nothing wrong with caring for one's family when they are in need. The way Joseph coached his brothers was based on his knowledge that Goshen in the Nile Delta was part of the most fertile land in Egypt. But I wonder if his motive was purely concern for the welfare of the Egyptians and his desire not to defile them.

The attitude of the pharaoh to the request is manifested in this text:

Pharaoh said to Joseph, "Your father and your brothers have come to you, and the land of Egypt is before you; settle your father and your brothers in the best part of the land. Let them live in Goshen. And if you know of any among them with special ability, put them in charge of my own livestock." Then Joseph brought his father Jacob in and presented him before Pharaoh. (47:5-7)

As a young Christian, I used to assume that Genesis 50 was followed by Exodus 1–2 with no time lapse. I assumed that right after Joseph died, the Jews started getting oppressed and Moses was born. Because the pharaohs at the time of Moses were evil, I assumed that all pharaohs were evil, including the pharaoh at the time of Joseph. Now I know that between the pharaoh who lived in Joseph's time and the pharaohs at the time of Moses, there must have been about twenty pharaohs over a period of about four hundred years. From this text in Genesis 47:5-7, we see that the pharaoh at the time of Joseph was a very good man who wanted to be generous to Joseph's family because he loved Joseph. Furthermore, because of his humility, he met Jacob and agreed to be blessed by him because of Jacob's old age.

In 47:11-12 we see how Joseph settled his family in the eastern part of the Nile Delta and provided them with land and food during the difficult time of starvation: "So Joseph settled his father and his brothers in Egypt and gave them property in the best part of the land, the district of Rameses, as Pharaoh directed. Joseph also provided his father and his brothers and all his father's household with food, according to the number of their children."

How did Joseph treat the Egyptians during his time as the ruler of Egypt? In Genesis 47 we see a different approach. He did not distribute to the hungry masses the food that was stored during the seven years of abundance. He had another plan:

> There was no food, however, in the whole region because the famine was severe; both Egypt and Canaan wasted away because of the famine. Joseph *collected all the money*. . . . When the money of the people of Egypt and Canaan was gone, all Egypt came to Joseph and said, "Give us food. Why should we die before your eyes? Our money is used up."
>
> "Then *bring your livestock*," said Joseph. "I will sell you food in exchange for your livestock, since your money is gone." So they brought their livestock to Joseph, and he gave them food in exchange for their horses. . . .
>
> When that year was over, they came to him the following year and said, "We cannot hide from our lord the fact that since our money is gone . . . there is nothing left for our lord

except our bodies and our land." . . .

So Joseph *bought all the land* in Egypt for Pharaoh . . . and Joseph *reduced the people to servitude,* from one end of Egypt to the other. However, he did not buy the *land of the priests,* because they received a regular allotment from Pharaoh. . . .

Now the *Israelites settled in Egypt* in the region of *Goshen.* They *acquired property* there and were fruitful and increased greatly in number. (verses 13-18,20-22,27, emphasis added)

It was God's will that the people should be helped through the years of starvation with wise planning. Otherwise God would have not given the dream regarding the future to the pharaoh. How the plans were carried through were left to Joseph. Instead of being fair, he cared for his family and made the pharaoh richer at the expense of the masses. If you were in Joseph's place as the prime minister, could you have come up with a plan that accomplished the purpose of the dream given by God without transforming a whole nation into slaves? Could you have done it without introducing the feudal system to one of the superpowers of the day?

Personally, I believe that Joseph set his family on a track where they ended up becoming an ethnocentric community four hundred years later. Perhaps his dysfunctional family background and his temperament played a role in the decisions he made. When the Israelites first came to Egypt, there were only sixty-six descendents of Jacob; they increased to become almost three million people. At that point, they constituted about 20 percent of the population of Egypt, and they owned land and property when the rest of the Egyptians were slaves.

Do you think they learned the language of the people? Were they concerned about the welfare of the Egyptians? Which of the three pictures that we covered earlier best describes them? Were they picture 1, 2, or 3?

In Exodus, we discover that four hundred years later

> Joseph and all his brothers and all that generation died, but the Israelites were fruitful and multiplied greatly and became exceedingly numerous, so that the land was filled with them.
>
> Then a new king, who did not know about Joseph, came to power in Egypt. "Look," he said to his people, "the Israelites have become much too numerous for us. Come, we must deal shrewdly with them or they will become even more numerous and, if war breaks out, will join our enemies, fight against us and leave the country." (1:6-10)

How were the people of God perceived by the Egyptians? Did they perceive them as picture 1, 2, or 3? It seems that even after four hundred years of living in Egypt, they were still viewed as foreigners. It was suspected that their loyalty to some future enemy would be stronger than their loyalty to the country that adopted them.

## THE EXILE

The people of God in Egypt were seen as an ethnocentric community of foreigners, and perhaps Joseph played an unconscious role in putting them on that set of tracks. In contrast, the people of God in Babylon went in a completely different direction and were a blessing to the nations.

As we look at the exile in Babylon, here are some historical details.

In 722 BC, the Assyrian army came and occupied the northern kingdom of Israel with its capital in Samaria. They practiced ethnic cleansing by taking many of the inhabitants of the northern kingdom to Assyria as slaves and bringing Assyrians to replace them. The

Assyrians and many other powers practiced such ethnic cleansings. By the time of Christ, so much mixing of races had taken place between the Jews in the northern kingdom and the Assyrians and others that the Samaritan Jews were perceived as an impure race by the Jews who lived in Judea, the southern kingdom.

In 722 BC, the Assyrian army continued their expansion until they reached Jerusalem and surrounded it. But they could not conquer the city. The Jews in Jerusalem believed that God miraculously delivered them. The Assyrian army had to retreat in a hurry back to Assyria. This was during the time of Isaiah the prophet.

Years later, in 586 BC, another army came and swept over Judea and surrounded Jerusalem. Many prophets at this time wore the cloak of patriotism, trying to emulate Isaiah's faith. They believed that as long as the temple was in Jerusalem, Jerusalem would not fall. The prophet Jeremiah declared that it was God's will for Jerusalem to surrender. Jeremiah was hated because in his message he did not take the patriotic line. God wanted to punish Judea, the southern kingdom, for its sins against Him over the years.

So in His sovereignty, God allowed the Babylonians to come, destroy the walls surrounding Jerusalem, and occupy the city. The temple was destroyed, and many parts of the city were burned. Most of the population of Jerusalem was taken as slaves to Babylon, and only the poorest of the poor were left in Jerusalem under a puppet king. The previous king was arrested along with his family. His sons were killed in front of him before the Babylonians plucked out his eyes and took him in chains to Babylon. That was how the period of exile in Babylon started. What a contrast to the beginning of the period when Jacob's family moved to Egypt!

Let us imagine a young man with the name Simon who lived in Jerusalem at that time. His parents were killed, and his sister was raped and left to die by a savage army officer and some of his soldiers. Simon was taken to Babylon as the personal slave of this savage Babylonian officer. In Babylon it was a struggle for Simon to know how to live and how to relate to the family of the man who owned him. At times he was allowed to attend some of the meetings that the Jews had. One of those meetings was a special occasion for the exiles in Babylon to listen to a letter sent by Jeremiah from Jerusalem. Simon had heard that the contents of the letter had to do with how the people of God should live and relate to the Babylonians. Here is an excerpt from the letter that Jeremiah wrote, taken from Jeremiah 29:4-7,10-14:

> This is what the LORD Almighty, the God of Israel, says to all those I carried into exile from Jerusalem to Babylon . . .

As Simon listened to the reading of this letter, he must have been struck by what Jeremiah had written. It was not the Babylonian army officer who was determining his destiny. God was the one in control of his destiny. The Babylonian officer must have thought he was the one who brought Simon to Babylon, but in reality it was God in His sovereign control who allowed Simon to be brought to Babylon.

> Build houses and settle down; plant gardens and eat what they produce. Marry and have sons and daughters; find wives for your sons and give your daughters in marriage, so that they too may have sons and daughters. Increase in number there; do not decrease.

Simon was reminded again that he was going to be in Babylon for a long time. It would not be just a couple of months before the Jews would return to Jerusalem; actually, it would be seventy years. He would be in Babylon for the rest of his life. Simon realized that he should not have a refugee mentality. Rather, God was telling him through Jeremiah to *settle down*, get married, and have children. He assumed that God was telling him to marry a Jewish woman rather than a Babylonian woman. The letter from Jeremiah continued:

> Also, seek the peace and prosperity of the city to which I have carried you into exile. Pray to the LORD for it, because if it prospers, you too will prosper.

This was too hard for Simon to swallow. God was telling him to seek the peace and prosperity of Babylon. How could he do that? It was the Babylonians who were responsible for the death of his family and the destruction of Jerusalem, yet now he was instructed to start praying for the prosperity of the man who owned him. If this man prospered, then Simon would prosper as well.

> This is what the LORD says: "When seventy years are completed for Babylon, I will come to you and fulfill my gracious promise to bring you back to this place. For I know the plans I have for you," declares the LORD, "plans to prosper you and not to harm you, plans to give you hope and a future. Then you will call upon me and come and pray to me, and I will listen to you. You will seek me and find me when you seek me with all your heart. I will be found by you," declares the LORD, "and will bring you back from captivity. I will gather you from all the nations and places where I have banished you," declares the LORD, "and will bring you back to the place from which I carried you into exile."

As Simon listened to the letter of Jeremiah, he realized that he needed to be farsighted. The issue at stake was not only his generation but many generations to come.

There were Jews in Babylon who did not practice what Jeremiah told them to do. They lived as picture 1, victims wishing they were back in Jerusalem. Yet there were others, like Daniel and his three friends, who lived like picture 3. They influenced kingdoms.

Daniel and his friends did not compromise their relationships with God; at the same time they did not marginalize themselves from the society in which God had placed them. Daniel, Hananiah, Mishael, and Azariah were given Babylonian names. Daniel was given the name Belteshazzar, Hananiah the name Shadrach, Mishael the name Meshach, and Azariah the name Abednego. Abednego means the slave or servant of Nego. Nego was a Babylonian god. Abednego did not get fixated on this new name or crippled by its awful meaning. He did not wonder whether he had actually become the slave of Nego. He knew that his God was the almighty God, the Creator of heaven and earth, and His name was Yahweh. He was even willing to be thrown in the furnace of fire because he loved his God Yahweh and was fully surrendered to Him.

Seventy years later, as God promised, the Jews were sent back to Jerusalem in groups. The books of Nehemiah, Ezra, and others deal with the return of the Jews. David Bosch in his book *Transforming Mission* pointed out that the biggest impact the Jews made on the nations was during the Exile and the period that followed. It was not during the time of the captivity in Egypt when they were mostly a picture 1 but in Babylon when they were mostly a picture 3.

Between Genesis 50 and Exodus 1 there is a period of four hundred years. Why did God not speak during those four hundred years when his people were living in Egypt? The beginning of the period and its end are covered, but not the bulk of the time. Were God's people worldly and therefore they lost their message? Did they become so ethnocentric that they forgot God and the purpose of their being? There are no books in the Old Testament that cover this period.

In contrast, the seventy years of exile in Babylon is covered broadly in the Old Testament. There are many books that talk about the events that led up to the Exile, and other books cover the Exile and the return to Judea. If we open our Bibles to the table of contents of the Old Testament, we see the following books that deal with the Exile: 2 Kings, 1 Chronicles, 2 Chronicles, Ezra, Nehemiah, Esther, Psalms, Isaiah, Jeremiah, Ezekiel, Daniel, and on and on. Can we come to the conclusion that when God's people are living picture 3, then there is a great deal of God's activity taking place and therefore God speaks in abundance?

## QUESTIONS FOR REFLECTION AND DISCUSSION

1. At the beginning of the chapter is this epigraph by a Jordanian Christian: "If they want to access our pure theology, they will need to learn our Christian vocabulary." What do you think of this quote in light of Ahmad's statements that follow?
2. In the past, have you ever seen Joseph portrayed the way he was presented in this chapter? What was new? What was strange?
3. What is the relevance of the periods of the Captivity and the Exile in our lives today?
4. Are Christians in your country perceived by the mainstream of society as an ethnocentric subculture? What could be the causes?
5. How do you think Christian minorities live in Muslim countries? How would Muslims in these countries perceive the Christians in terms of pictures 1, 2, and 3?

# CHAPTER 9

# ISOLATED AND WATERED DOWN

*Muslims are trying to invade us from all directions. If we are not strong, we will be taken over by the Muslims.*

— AN ETHIOPIAN CHRISTIAN

In a private conversation, Ahmad asked me, *"Why is it that many Christians in Egypt live with a fortress mentality? I notice the same mentality here in America. The Religious Right is perceived with suspicion by mainstream Americans."*

In the previous chapter we looked at two great periods in the Old Testament, the captivity in Egypt and the exile in Babylon. The people of God while in Egypt were very much picture 1 and perhaps picture 2 as well. They failed to be picture 3 — being in the world and yet not of the world. They failed to be a blessing to the nations. This was true to the extent that the Egyptians in Exodus 1 were convinced that if an enemy attacked Egypt, the Israelites who had lived in Egypt for four hundred years would still side with the enemy against the Egyptians. In contrast, the people of God in Babylon during the Exile were very much picture 3. Daniel and his friends influenced kings.

In this chapter we will look at the implications of the study of these two periods on our lives in the world today. I will share extensively from the life of one of my personal friends in Egypt, Samuel, and how the lessons of the captivity in Egypt and the exile in Babylon have been put into practice in contemporary Egypt. The implications of the lessons learned from these two periods apply not only to Muslim countries but to every country in the world.

Just to keep them in mind, here are the three pictures again with a brief summary of each.

Picture 1: Isolation. Holy huddle. Fortress mentality.

Picture 2: A life of compromise. The messenger lost the message.

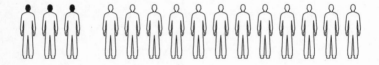

Picture 3: In the world, yet not of the world. Salt and light. A blessing to the nations.

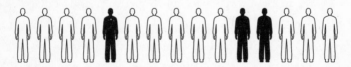

## Isolation Versus Being in the World

From 1975 to 1990, our family lived in Egypt. At one time we started pursuing the possibility of staying in the country for the rest of our lives. But God had other plans for us, and we moved to the States in January 1991.* During our years in Egypt, one of my best friends was a man named Samuel. Samuel was an evangelical Coptic Christian.**

During our first year in Egypt when I came to know Samuel, he was in a Bible study with us. He worked as a teacher in a government school that was just a five-minute walk from his apartment. His work at school started at eight and finished at noon. He was paid a very small salary. The rest of each day he spent at his church, where he became the hub of most of the activities. He was even invited to attend the elders' meetings although he was not an elder at that time.

One day Samuel came to visit me and told me that he had a job offer to work in a large steel factory. The salary was great, but there was a major downfall to the job. He would work six days a week starting each day at seven and finishing at five. Furthermore, it would take an hour to commute to work in the factory bus and an hour to return home. In essence, it was a twelve-hour-a-day job. So Samuel hesitated to accept the offer.

I asked him, "Samuel, are you planning to get married one of these days?" When he responded in the affirmative, I asked him why he was thinking about turning down that new job considering that it offered a much better salary. Very soon I learned that his concern was his personal ministry at his church, which he would have to leave. So we talked about ministry at work, especially in light of the fact that more

---

\* In September 1990, I was expelled from Egypt, blacklisted, and given ten days to leave the country.

\*\* Coptic is the Greek word for "Egyptian." There are Coptic Orthodox and Coptic Protestants.

than 90 percent of the people working in the factory were Muslims. We agreed together that if he took this new job, the people he trained at the church would carry the responsibility and would grow in the process. So Samuel left me that day, promising that he would pray about the job offer.

A few days later, he and another Christian were hired to work in that factory. The next morning they were supposed to meet the factory bus at five minutes before six. The other Christian hired from Samuel's church, Maged, tended to be a picture 1 Christian. When the bus came it was three-quarters full, and Maged got onto the bus first. He greeted people in the bus by saying, "Good morning," using Arab Christian terminology. No one responded, and no one wanted him to sit next to him. So Maged walked to the back of the bus and sat in the last row alone. Then Samuel got onto the bus and with a big smile greeted the factory workers with the Arab Muslim greeting, *"Asalamu 'alaykum"* ("Peace to you"). They all responded by saying, *"Wa alikum salam wa ramhatu Allah wa barakatuh"* ("And peace be to you and God's mercy and His blessings"). People wanted Samuel to sit next to them, so he sat next to a Muslim. In fifteen seconds, each of the two men, Maged and Samuel, communicated a great deal about themselves.

On a Friday a couple of weeks after he started working at the factory, Samuel came to visit me, and I asked him about the new job. He told me that the opportunities for evangelism were endless, but since he started his job, he was not reading his Bible. He used to have a morning quiet time, but since he started working at the factory, he could hardly get up in the morning, and at night when he tried to read his Bible, he fell asleep out of exhaustion. So as we talked about it, he decided to have his quiet time in the factory bus on his way to work. The next morning he took with him his little New Testament and was reading in the gospel of Mark. The Muslim sitting next to him was peeking to see what Samuel was reading. So Samuel cried out privately to God, *Lord, can't I have fifteen minutes on my own?* Then he asked forgiveness of God for his impatience and lack of love. He turned to the man next to him, told him that he was reading the life of Christ, and asked him whether he would like him to read it aloud. The man was eager to hear, so Samuel had his quiet time with a Muslim that morning. From that point on, some mornings he had his quiet time on his own, and other times the trip to the factory started as a quiet time with one of the factory workers and ended as an opportunity for sharing the good news about Jesus.

Several weeks later Samuel was sharing with me the excitement he was experiencing in his job and the many opportunities he had to love Muslims and connect with them. He told me, though, that since he started his new job at the factory, he never reviewed his verses. He used to memorize a couple of verses each week and review the rest of the verses on a weekly basis, but he hadn't since he started that job. By the end of our conversation, he came up with an idea that blew my mind. Samuel is fearless, and his plan was inspired by his courageous attitude. He told me that they have three breaks during the day: at ten, noon, and three. The idea he had was to review his verses during the ten o'clock break and to ask any factory worker sitting next to him to check him on his verses. Since the majority of the workers were Muslims, I wondered about the wisdom of his plan.

A few weeks later I asked him about his verses and how his plan was going. He told me that the next day after our time together, he took with him the leather packet that contained his verses written on little cards. He gave the packet to a Muslim he didn't know who was sitting next to him. He explained to him that on the cards were verses from the Tawrat and Injil and asked him if he would be willing to check him for any mistakes he was making. The man took the responsibility very seriously, and every time Samuel made a mistake, he would stop him and ask him to repeat the verse five times. Samuel told me that he had never reviewed his verses so thoroughly before.

In his later attempts, sometimes the fifteen-minute break started with review and ended up as an evangelism opportunity. One time, though, when a man realized that the packet contained verses from the Bible, he dropped the packet to the ground and asked God to forgive him for defiling himself. If I experienced something like that, I would have questioned the wisdom of asking Muslims to check me on my verses. Samuel's response was, "So what? This is a quick way to find out those who are open-minded and those who are fanatical."

A few months after Samuel started working at the factory, the month of Ramadan came. It was in the midst of summer. Because Muslims follow the lunar calendar, which is shorter than our calendar, the month of Ramadan varies from year to year. At times it comes in the spring; at other times it comes in the winter or the summer. During Ramadan, Muslims fast, without food or drink, from sunrise to sunset. When Ramadan comes in the winter, fasting is relatively easy. The days are short, and those fasting do not struggle much with thirst. But when Ramadan comes in the summer, the days are very long and the need for water is intense. Samuel, along with the other Christians who worked at the factory, went in a little room to eat and drink during the three breaks, while the Muslims were outside in the heat of the sun. Every Muslim knew what those Christians were doing in that room, and they hated them for it.

Samuel joined the Christians for a couple of days but then felt that there was something wrong in what he was doing. So he asked God for direction and then came up with a plan. He decided to fast with the Muslims, but not in the exact way they were fasting. He was not a Muslim, but he wanted to be "like Muslims" to win Muslims as friends and ultimately to Christ (see 1 Corinthians 9:19-23). He decided to eat and drink just before he went to catch the factory bus at six each morning. As soon as he returned home at six in the evening, the food would be ready for him. From six to six he decided not to eat or drink. Muslims, in contrast, would wake up at four to eat before sunrise and would not eat in the evening till sunset, which was about seven thirty during that time of the year. Samuel wanted to communicate to the Muslims who had become his friends that he was fasting because he loved them rather than for the purpose of trying to earn the love of God.

One day one of the engineers working with him observed that Samuel was no longer going to that room where the Christians ate and drank. He asked him, "Are you fasting?" Samuel said, "Yes." "Like us?" the man asked. So Samuel explained to him that he was fasting from six to six. So the engineer asked him, "Is this the Orthodox fast?" Samuel told him that when the Orthodox fast they abstain from certain foods. So the engineer concluded, "Then this must be a Protestant fast." Samuel told him that Protestants do not fast. So the man asked him, "Then why are you fasting?" Samuel then had the opportunity to explain to him that when God loves us He does not throw His message from heaven like a basketball and hope that we will catch it. He explained to him how God loved us through Christ as He visited us on earth.

A few days later, it was a very hot day. At about two in the afternoon, Samuel was walking in the heat of the sun with two Muslim engineers when he fainted. The two men carried him into the shade and seated him on a chair while many came around to watch. One of the two engineers ran and got a jug of water along with a glass. They poured water on Samuel's face until he regained consciousness. Then the engineer filled the glass again and said to Samuel, "We know that you love us. We want you to drink right now, fast or no fast."

Samuel was one of my models of how to be a picture 3 Christian. He was in the world, yet he was not of the world. When God looked at his daily life, He must have looked at him with a smile.

## CRIPPLING FEAR

The temptation for any Christians living among the mainstream is either to isolate themselves or to become colorless and lose the message. In an earlier chapter, I shared with you how my friends in Egypt and I studied several themes in the Scriptures, all the way from Genesis to Revelation. One of the themes we studied was What is the good news of the gospel to Muslims? At the end of the study the team tried to identify the major issue that prevented them from fully being what God wanted them to be in this area. They concluded that it was *fear*. So sometime later over a period of several months, they studied the subject of fear in all the Scriptures, and God delivered many of them from the consequences of crippling fear.

Years before the study on fear, I visited Cyprus,* and Samuel came to spend a few days there with me. We discussed the situation of the ministry in Egypt and came to the conclusion that one of the biggest weapons the Devil uses is the weapon of fear. It can paralyze God's children. We thought of mutual friends who had been cornered by the Devil. It felt as though the Devil forced these Christians to stand in a corner while he drew a line on the floor and commanded them not to cross it. It must break the heart of God to see His children cornered by the Devil.

As we continued our sharing and praying, I asked Samuel, "What are you afraid of?" By this time, Samuel was married and had three young children. He said, "I am afraid that the secret police might come one night at two or three in the morning, knock at the door of our apartment, and ask me to go with them to their headquarters in Cairo for a short interview. I know it will not be a short interview but imprisonment for months or years."

---

* Cyprus is an hour's flight from Cairo, Egypt. We met in Cyprus because I was blacklisted and was not allowed to visit Egypt.

So I asked him again, "What are you afraid of?" He told me that he was not very worried about his family because his church assured him that they would take good care of them. Then he told me that his wife might get lucky and find him in the first prison she visited; or it might take her months to find him by asking for him in every prison in Egypt, and they are all over the country. Then he told me that the food offered in prisons is of terrible quality. Prisoners usually eat only what their relatives bring to them. At the same time, Samuel assured me that he was not really worried about the food. He knew that he could establish deep relationships with fellow prisoners and they would share their food with him.

So I asked him a third time, "Then what are you afraid of?" He thought for a while and then said, "I am afraid that I will get imprisoned so suddenly that I will go to prison without my reading glasses, daily medications, a toothbrush, and my Bible." As a result of our conversation, he gave a living will regarding his family to a close friend, and he decided to pack a little case and put in it pajamas, a toothbrush and toothpaste, a pair of reading glasses, a Bible, and medications that are kept up to date. That small case was packed in the early nineties, and through all the years he lived in Egypt he did not need to use it. The sting of fear was broken once Samuel identified the exact source of his fear and addressed it.*

In 2004, Samuel was asked to report to the secret police office at a set time on a certain day. People who get interrogated usually arrive on time or early. Then they sit for hours waiting to be interrogated. The secret police purposefully keep the people waiting as they struggle with anxiety and fear. By the time they finally get called in to be interrogated, they are ready to cooperate. Fear prepares them to say everything.

---

\* Samuel moved with his family to the States in 2006 and now has regional responsibilities and a TV ministry aimed at the entire Arab world, rather than directing the ministry exclusively in Egypt.

Samuel told me that before he went to be interrogated, he dressed to the nines, as if he were going to a wedding. He purposefully arrived half an hour late, and he sat on a chair with one leg over the other reading the newspaper. Shortly afterward, he was invited in, and they tried to terrify him by using various approaches. To make the story short, nothing worked.*

The next strategy they used was to interrogate his friends and those who worked with him. Every single one of them was asked, "What do you know about Samuel?" Some were not shaken, but others were cornered by the Devil through fear and did not work with Samuel anymore in the future.

In July 2005, my wife and I visited Egypt for a couple of weeks with a special one-time visa. During that time we attended a conference. One of the best messages I have ever heard, given by Samuel, was on the topic of fear.

It is a challenge to live in the world and not be of the world. It is easy for us to isolate ourselves, live in our subculture, and become immune to the needs of people around us. It is also easy to water down our message in order to face less persecution or to protect our lives from additional burdens. Samuel was a model for me in living on the balance beam.

## Questions for Reflection and Discussion

1. Go back to the beginning of the chapter. What do you think of Ahmad's observations about Christians in Egypt and in America? What do you think of the statement made by the Ethiopian Christian?

---

* Samuel was not doing anything illegal, and the secret police knew it. They basically wanted to intimidate him so he would stop his ministry to Muslims.

2. Who are your models of people who are in the world but not of the world?

3. Describe how they avoid being picture 1 and 2.

4. What crippling fears do Christians in your country have?

# CHAPTER 10

# THE POWER OF PARADIGMS

*We know what the real needs of Muslims are. They need to believe in Christ and be saved.*

— an Indonesian Christian

Ahmad told me, *"I do not understand why I have a hard time communicating with Christians in America about my real and felt needs. These good Christians whom I love tend to address what they assume to be my real and felt needs without asking me what they really are."*

A young American university student, Nancy, was walking back to her dorm on a dark night. She was assaulted by a young man who duct-taped her mouth so that she could not scream and then raped her. When he finished, he tied her to a tree and ran away. Later on she was found, taken to the emergency room, and treated for the injuries she suffered. The ordeal was horrific. She experienced physical pain, shame, humiliation, guilt, and, above all, a sense of being filthy. During the horrible and painful rape experience, for a very brief moment, she felt a sense of sexual pleasure.

Later, she shared with the counselor at the university her experience in great detail. Tearfully, she confided how she felt ashamed as she lost her virginity. She told also about her guilt over the brief moment of sexual pleasure she had experienced. Above all, she shared in great length how she felt, and still feels, filthy.

During the counseling session, the counselor latched on to the guilt factor and did not pay much attention to the other layers of Nancy's experience. When the session finished, the counselor was encouraged by a job well done. She had succeeded in assuring Nancy that she should not feel guilty about her brief moment of sexual pleasure. Nancy looked at the counseling session differently, however. She still felt very filthy.

Many times when we connect with Muslims, we assume that we are on the same wavelength as they are, when in reality we are not connecting with them at all. The counselor thought she had done a great job as she focused on the issue of guilt. She assumed guilt was the major felt need that Nancy had; therefore, once guilt was dealt with, the problem was solved. Nancy's experience and felt needs were very different, however. Her biggest need was to know how to deal with her feeling of being filthy. In other words, her deepest problem was not guilt but shame and defilement.

## DIFFERENT PARADIGMS

My wife and I invited a Muslim friend of ours to go with us to watch the movie *The Passion of the Christ*. Before we went to the movie, we visited her at her home. I wanted to share with her the gospel so that when she saw the movie she would be able to see the crucifixion and the resurrection of Christ within the whole context of the good news of the gospel. So I shared the gospel with her in my traditional approach, presenting God in His holiness and righteousness. Then I talked about sin and its penalty and what Jesus accomplished on the cross in His resurrection.

But what was different in my presentation this time was my attempt to present sin not only on the basis of guilt and righteousness, but also on the basis of shame and honor, defilement (*najasa*) and becoming clean (*tahara*), fear and power. When I finished the presentation, to our surprise and joy, the woman responded by saying, "Oh, how I long to be clean!" She did not say, "Oh, how I long to be forgiven" because she was not feeling guilty. Her felt need was not guilt but the defilement on the inside, which we call depravity.*

A couple of years ago I read a book with the title *Honor and Shame: Unlocking the Door*, written by Roland Muller.[1] In his book Muller speaks of four main paradigms:** the guilt/righteousness paradigm, the shame/honor paradigm, the defilement/clean paradigm, and the fear/power paradigm. Muller believes that the guilt/righteousness paradigm exists in the Christian West, while the shame/honor paradigm and the defilement/clean paradigm exist mostly in Muslim countries.

Actually, the shame/honor paradigm exists not only in Muslim countries but spreads all the way from North Africa in the West to Korea and Japan in the East. The fear/power paradigm exists in the minds of folk Muslims all over the Muslim world and in some African countries where some people are occupied with the demonic and with magic.

Muller accurately says that the Bible covers all these paradigms.

---

\*    The Arabic word for being unclean, *najasa*, means filthy and repulsive. There is no politically correct word for the word *unclean* in Arabic.

\*\*  A paradigm is similar to a worldview, which is the lens through which we look at reality. It is our distinct perspective.

So the challenge we face is learning to present the gospel *with all four paradigms* in mind, *starting* with the paradigm appropriate to the person we are connecting with.

Many times we Christians tend to shrink down the good news of the gospel to the assurance that we can be completely and permanently forgiven (guilt/righteousness or legal paradigm). Are there other dimensions to the good news of the gospel? Does the gospel give us the assurance that we can be completely and permanently cleansed from our filth and defilement? Furthermore, does the gospel promise that we can be completely and permanently unshackled from all our fears? Is it easier for us to believe that we are completely forgiven than to believe that we are entirely clean? If we present the gospel only with the guilt/righteousness paradigm, we are presenting a truncated gospel. The Bible is loaded with all four paradigms, but for various reasons, we Christians, especially in the West, have been trained to take notice only of the guilt/righteousness paradigm. Here are some reasons:

1. Paul's letters are loaded with legal terminology such as guilt, penalty of sin, judgment, and justification.
2. Some of the early church fathers were not only theologians but also lawyers, such as Quintus Tertullian (ca. 160–225) and Aurelius Prudentius (ca. 348–405). Not only that, but some of the Reformers, such as Calvin, were also lawyers in addition to being theologians. So our commentaries are loaded with legal terminology.
3. The famous tools for evangelism that were created in America and spread all over the world through organizations and mission agencies all use legal terminology. The "Four Spiritual Laws" is just one example.
4. The famous evangelists whom God used in the twentieth century in the lives of many people used the guilt/righteousness paradigm. Billy Graham is the prime example.

5. Perhaps most of us reading this book, as we remember the message we believed that transformed our lives, would come to the conclusion that the message was based on the legal or guilt/righteousness paradigm.

6. Christian commentaries around the world are colored by the Western culture. English is the international language, the church in the West tends to be wealthy, and there is an abundance of well-known Bible scholars in the West. Therefore, it is more likely that a commentary written in English by an American Bible scholar using the guilt/righteousness paradigm would be translated into other languages than a commentary written in Arabic by an Egyptian Bible scholar using the shame/honor paradigm.

For these reasons and others, we have developed some blind spots when we read our Bibles. This blindness influences not only how we understand and present the good news of the gospel but also how we interpret many texts in the Scriptures. Even as an Arab who has lived in the Middle East most of my life, I have found that because of my education, I tend to wear Western lenses when I read my Bible. My teacher and friend Dr. Kenneth Bailey helped me become more aware of my Western lenses and dared me to put on my Arab lenses.[2] The town where I grew up, before the era of electricity, telephones, radios, and TVs, is probably much closer to the culture of the Bible than what we picture. I have an abundance of illustrations as well that add depth and breadth to what we can discover in the Bible if we look through the lenses of other paradigms. Here are a couple of them that Kenneth Bailey opened my eyes to.

## BLIND SPOTS

In one of his parables, Jesus said,

> Suppose one of you has a friend, and he goes to him at midnight and says, "Friend, lend me three loaves of bread, because a friend of mine on a journey has come to me, and I have nothing to set before him."
>
> Then the one inside answers, "Don't bother me. The door is already locked, and my children are with me in bed. I can't get up and give you anything." I tell you, though he will not get up and give him the bread because he is his friend, yet because of the man's boldness [*anaideia*] he will get up and give him as much as he needs. (Luke 11:5-8)

The Greek word *anaideia* in verse 8 can have different shades of meanings. The translators try to choose the closest to the truth. The ISV translates it as "persistence," the ASV translates it as "importunity," and the NIV translates it as "boldness." Another shade to the word means "shamelessness," which has to do with honor. Which one is the closest to the truth? The historical cultural context could offer some answers.

Let us try to imagine this story taking place in a Judean village at the time of Christ. There are no telephones, no electricity, no McDonald's. A guest arrives unannounced at midnight, and he is hungry. The host and his wife are embarrassed that they do not have bread, the main staple, because the next day was the day for baking fresh bread. So this host goes to his friend and neighbor to borrow bread. There are no phones or doorbells, so he knocks on the door. It is dark because there are no electric lights in the street. The man upstairs peeks from the window and sees a man holding a lantern in front of his door. He can't see who this man is because the light of the lantern is not bright enough. So he shouts out, "Who is it?"

The man by the door shouts out, "Friend, lend me three loaves of bread, because a friend of mine on a journey has come to me, and I have nothing to set before him." The man upstairs recognizes the voice of the man who is knocking at the door. Can the man upstairs shout back, "Don't bother me. The door is already locked, and my children are with me in bed. I can't get up and give you anything"? By now most of the neighbors are awake and are curious and listening. From the voices, they know who the two men are. If he turns his neighbor away, how could the man upstairs face his other neighbors the next day when hospitality has such a high value in that culture?

When the word *anaideia* is understood in the context of the shame/honor paradigm, translating it as "persistence" does not make sense. Can you imagine the man downstairs persisting in knocking at the door after the humiliation of rejection? This is impossible! The parable is about honor and shame rather than persistence. There is a parable that talks about persistence, but it is not this one.* What is the point that Jesus was communicating through this parable? Not persistence but boldness, as the NIV translates it. Jesus was saying that we can count on God because He will be true to His promises. Because of His honor He will answer our prayers.

Before we look at another passage, we need to remember that when travelers arrive at a village in the Middle East, they stay with relatives or friends. If they do not know anyone in that village, they might stay in the guesthouse of a well-known, rich, and hospitable person in the village. Guests come unannounced.

In another passage in Luke, we have a narrative of the birth of Christ:

---

* The unjust judge and the persistence of the widow in Luke 18:1-8.

In those days Caesar Augustus issued a decree that a census should be taken of the entire Roman world. (This was the first census that took place while Quirinius was governor of Syria.) And everyone went to his own town to register.

So Joseph also went up from the town of Nazareth in Galilee to Judea, to Bethlehem the town of David, because he belonged to the house and line of David. He went there to register with Mary, who was pledged to be married to him and was expecting a child. While they were there, the time came for the baby to be born, and she gave birth to her firstborn, a son. She wrapped him in cloths and placed him in a manger, because there was no room for them in the inn. (2:1-7)

Though Joseph lived in Nazareth, he was originally from Bethlehem. Because of the decree passed by Caesar Augustus regarding the census, Joseph had to return to Bethlehem with his betrothed, Mary, who was pregnant in her ninth month. The distance was ninety miles over very hilly country. The trip must have taken several days. Joseph and Mary were not the only ones who went to Bethlehem; all the original inhabitants of that town had to go back to get registered in the census. It was a great reunion for all the Bethlehemites. Verse 7 says, "She gave birth to her firstborn, a son. She wrapped him in cloths and placed him in a manger, because there was no room for them in the inn [*kataluma*]."

The Greek word *kataluma* means the upper or guest room of a home, and it is usually reserved for guests. We see the word *kataluma* appearing in Luke 22:11 and Mark 14:14 in reference to Jesus' celebrating the Last Supper with His disciples in the *kataluma*, or the upper room. There is another Greek word for the word *inn*, which is *pando*, and we see it also in the gospel of Luke in the parable of the Good Samaritan: "He went to him and bandaged his wounds, pouring on oil and wine. Then he put the man on his own donkey, took him to an inn [*pando*] and took care of him" (10:34). In this passage about the birth of Christ, why do translators insist on translating *kataluma* as "inn" instead of "upper room"? Why did Luke use the word *kataluma* when he could have used the word *pando*? If we look at Luke 2:7 again and translate *kataluma* as "upper room," will the verse make sense? "She gave birth to her firstborn, a son. She wrapped him in cloths and placed him in a manger, because there was no room for them in the *upper room*."

When I look at this verse through my Arab lenses and through the help of Dr. Bailey, it amazes me to think that Joseph returned to his hometown and did not find one relative who could offer him hospitality! The town was full of relatives because everyone had returned to Bethlehem. Mary was in a very unusual circumstance, ready to give birth, and yet not one person offered hospitality! To put this in perspective, consider what Abraham did with the "three strangers" who visited him: "Then he ran to the herd and selected a choice, tender calf and gave it to a servant, who hurried to prepare it. He then brought some curds and milk and the calf that had been prepared, and set these before them" (Genesis 18:7-8).

Could it be that the translators of Luke 2:7 were confused by the word *manger* and assumed that it must have been a stable? Could it be that they were not familiar with the fact that animals were brought into the lower section of the split-level living room area at night for safety and for protection against the elements? Could it be that these translators were not aware of the fact that every morning the animals were taken out to the courtyard and their place was cleaned thoroughly? Could it be that they were not aware of the fact that mangers separated the lower-level place of the animals from the slightly upper level of the living room? That living room was a bedroom at night and a living room during the day. The upper or guest room was a room on the second floor of the house or annexed to the living room.

I understand Luke 2:7 to mean that because there was no place in the guest room, Mary gave birth in the living/bedroom, and the baby Jesus was placed on a clean sheet in a manger since the animals were outside. I can imagine the room was packed with busy women who were close to the host family, including a midwife. I can imagine the men waiting in another room with Joseph anticipating the birth of the expected baby. The guest room must have been occupied by other guests who were older in age.

In this Eastern context of honor/shame, Luke 2:7 can have a completely new meaning and a new appreciation. God, in the person of Christ, came to earth and dwelt among us. He was not secluded from humanity in a stable; he was born in a room in a house full of people. How many Christmas songs and poems need to be rewritten if this interpretation is accurate? Are we missing out on seeing the beauty of the depth and the breadth of the Scriptures because we look only though our familiar lenses? For the past several years during my study of the Scriptures, I have been looking not only through the lens of the guilt/righteousness paradigm but also through the lenses of the shame/honor, defilement/clean, and fear/power paradigms.

In this chapter we started out with the story of the university student who was raped and whose counselor failed to help her at a deep level because the counselor was not aware of the student's real felt need. Then we looked at four paradigms, or lenses, that exist in the Bible, namely the guilt/righteousness or legal paradigm, the shame/honor paradigm, the defilement/clean paradigm, and the fear/power paradigm. We also examined the fact that when we look at the Scriptures only through the guilt/righteousness paradigm, we end up having blind spots and miss out on the rich tapestry of the Scriptures.

In the next chapter, we will examine the four paradigms further and illustrate from the Scriptures the breadth and depth of the gospel as we try to understand the Muslims' worldview and connect with them at deeper levels.

## QUESTIONS FOR REFLECTION AND DISCUSSION

1. Go back to the beginning of the chapter. What do you think of the statement made by Ahmad regarding his felt needs? What do you think of the statement made by the Indonesian Christian?

2. Have you ever been given answers to questions you are not asking? How did you feel? What does listening to people require if we are to discover their real felt needs?

3. Can you think of passages in the Bible that speak clearly about
   a. the shame/honor paradigm?
   b. the defilement/clean paradigm?
   c. the fear/power paradigm?

4. Consider the story of Lot in Genesis 19:1-8. His house was bombarded by a horde of homosexuals who demanded to have his guests. Lot offered them his daughters in exchange: "Look, I have two daughters who have never slept with a man. Let me bring them out to you, and you can do what you like with them. But don't do anything to these men, for they have come under the protection of my roof" (verse 8). Why did he do that?

# CHAPTER 11

# SHAME, DEFILEMENT, AND FEAR

*The facts of the gospel as they are summarized in book-lets such as the "Four Spiritual Laws" should be suffi-cient for anyone around the world if they truly want to know the truth.*

— A Nigerian Christian

In presenting to me the Muslims' worldview, Ahmad said, *"When I talk with you it feels like you are laying a guilt trip on me. Does your message have anything to say to me about my shame, my defilement, and my fear?"*

On one of my trips to a third world Muslim country, I was invited to speak to a group of about forty Muslim villagers. Two-thirds of them were men and one-third women. They ranged from the age of twenty-seven to sixty-five. These people chose to come to the capital city in a bus in response to the invitation of the Christian development agency that was doing microprojects to help them succeed in life. These people had heard very little about Christ and the Bible because of limited freedom by the development agency staff.

Because I am an Arab and have read the Qur'an in the original language, I had a platform with these people. When I arrived at the meeting room, it was filled with forty guests who were sitting on the floor in a U shape, the women on one side and the men on the other two sides. There were two chairs facing these people, one for me and the other for my interpreter. I had assumed that I would have one hour to speak, but when I got there I discovered that I was being given two full hours. I had mixed feelings. I felt honored for being given that privilege; at the same time I felt sad for these people sitting on the floor for two whole hours. If I had to sit on the floor like they did, I would be crippled because of my lower back problems.

Before coming to that meeting I had prayed and thought about how to present the good news of the gospel to them using their own paradigms. I decided not to use texts that I have used in the past. Instead, I decided to use Mark chapter 5 with its three very relevant stories.

## THE FIRST STORY

The first story in Mark 5:1-20 is about a wild, demon-possessed man by the name of Legion — a reference to the many demons that possessed him. This man was very strong and lived among the tombs. We read that "no one could bind him any more, not even with a chain. . . . No one was strong enough to subdue him. Night and day among the tombs and in the hills he would cry out and cut himself with stones" (verses 3-5).

He became an outcast not only from his family and extended family but also from the people in the town. I can imagine the horror stories that must have developed as part of the folklore that surrounded that man. It was quite a setting for these horror stories: the graveyard and the tombs at night, the breaking chains, a demon-possessed man crying out. Even the bravest of the brave must have avoided that area of town, especially at night.

As I got into this story I could sense that I was connecting well with these forty villagers. Folk Islam exists in every Muslim country in the world. It is the religion of the poor and the uneducated. The theology of folk Islam comes from three sources—a little from the Qur'an, a bit more from Muslim traditions, and a great deal from folk superstitions. According to Bill Musk in his book *The Unseen Face of Islam*, folk Islam considers the spirits (*jinn*) a separate species of beings. They are created out of fire (see Surah 55:15) and are somewhere between angels and men. They belong to the world of spirits, yet they live within the human domain. They form three categories: good jinn, evil jinn, and neutral jinn. Fear of jinn, or the desire to subdue them and use their services, is very big in folk Islam. Jinn exist in certain places, such as graveyards, and afflict people during certain activities, such as sexual intercourse or defecation.

As I got into the details of the story and as I reached its climax, the people's eyes were wide open when they saw Jesus' power over the demonic. They were amazed that the demons recognized who Jesus was and were afraid of Him. The demon-possessed man came to Jesus, and, as the Bible says, "He ran and fell on his knees in front of him. He shouted at the top of his voice, 'What do you want with me, Jesus, Son of the Most High God? Swear to God that you won't torture me!'" (verses 6-7).

Everyone in that room knew that this demon-possessed man was worthless. He was a menace to the town and to the neighboring villages. Why did Jesus give him worth and cast the demons out and into the pigs? Why did He treat him with compassion and give him a purpose for living? The source of menace became a bearer of the good news about Jesus in that town.

Through this first story, I was able to present Jesus to them through their paradigm of fear/power. They saw Jesus having the authority and power over the jinn and the demonic in a visible manner when the demons went into the pigs. This story prepared them for the next powerful story in Mark chapter 5.

## THE SECOND STORY

The second story in Mark 5:21-34 is about Jesus' willingness to heal a hemorrhaging woman. Jesus crossed over to the other side of the lake along with His disciples in a boat, and very soon a crowd gathered around him. A man by the name of Jairus came to him and fell at His feet. He pleaded to Jesus to go with him to his home to heal his twelve-year-old daughter, who was very sick. Jesus had compassion on this man and decided to go with him. So Jesus, along with the crowds gathered around him, started walking with Jairus toward his town. But Jesus was interrupted. We learn that "a woman was there who had been subject to bleeding for twelve years. She had suffered a great deal under the care of many doctors and had spent all she had, yet instead of getting better she grew worse" (verses 25-26).

What was the worth of a woman with this kind of disease in a Jewish town? To start with, she was in a very bad state physically, having an extraordinary menstruation — a nonstop period — for twelve years. Can you imagine her daily laundry? Furthermore, it seems that her doctors had given up on her after she spent all her wealth trying to get healed. So physically she was depleted, and financially she was bankrupt. In a nutshell, she was desperate. We go on to read, "When she heard about Jesus, she came up behind him in the crowd and touched his cloak, because she thought, 'If I just touch his clothes, I will be healed'" (verses 27-28).

How could she dare approach Jesus, penetrating the crowd around Him? I turned to the book of Leviticus and read to the forty villagers passages from chapters 12 and 15:

> The LORD said to Moses, "Say to the Israelites: 'A woman who becomes pregnant and gives birth to a son will be ceremonially unclean for seven days, just as she is unclean during her monthly period. . . . Then the woman must wait thirty-three days to be purified from her bleeding. She must not touch anything sacred or go to the sanctuary until the days of her purification are over. If she gives birth to a daughter, for two weeks the woman will be unclean, as during her period. Then she must wait sixty-six days to be purified from her bleeding.'" (12:1-5)

Even before I got into Leviticus 15, I could sense the presence of God in a special way in that room. The people were spellbound by the relevance of what was being read. I could sense how the women especially were identifying with this poor woman and her pain of being rejected because of her uncleanness. So I continued reading, this time in Leviticus 15:

> When a woman has her regular flow of blood, the impurity of her monthly period will last seven days, and anyone who touches her will be unclean till evening. Anything she lies on during her period will be unclean, and anything she sits on will be unclean. Whoever touches her bed must wash his clothes and bathe with water, and he will be unclean till evening. Whoever touches anything she sits on must wash his clothes and bathe with water, and he will be unclean till evening. Whether it is the bed or anything she was sitting on,

when anyone touches it, he will be unclean till evening. (verses
19-23)

It felt as though I did not need to say anything. These villagers
understood the challenge this woman had to face in order to reach
out and touch Jesus. What if one of the men in the crowd knew who
she was and confronted her in public because she defiled him? What if
she was beaten by these men who were all around Jesus? What if Jesus
Himself became defiled by her and rejected her as everybody else did?

Muslims practice ceremonial washings or ablutions, when possible, before they pray the ceremonial prayer. In a certain set manner,
the Muslim washes his hands, face, feet, and other parts of his body. A
man after doing the ablutions cannot shake hands with unclean people
or he will lose the purity he has gained. If he approaches God in the
ceremonial prayer while defiled, deep within his soul he knows that he
is unclean and therefore God does not listen to his prayer.

I remember a good friend of mine, who comes from a Muslim
background and loves Jesus, telling me how he felt sad for Muslim
women. He told me that during the month of Ramadan, everybody
in his family fasted, including his wife, even during her menstruation
period. Deep in her soul she knew that during those days when she was
"defiled," her fasting didn't count. So when the month of Ramadan
was over and everybody was enjoying the celebration of good food that
lasted for days, that poor woman could not celebrate. She was on her
own, still fasting to make up for the days that didn't count because she
had her period.

I sensed God was helping me connect with these villagers in a
very deep way. The story of this woman in Mark 5 was addressing
their felt need of longing to be clean so that they would be acceptable to God. In Mark 7 Jesus addressed this longing with these words:
"What comes out of a man is what makes him 'unclean.' For from

within, out of men's hearts, come evil thoughts, sexual immorality, theft, murder, adultery, greed, malice, deceit, lewdness, envy, slander, arrogance and folly. All these evils come from inside and make a man 'unclean'" (verses 20-23).

Jesus pointed out that it is not a matter of ceremonial washings and cleaning oneself on the outside. The big problem is not our *outer defilement* but our *inner depravity*. Does the good news of the gospel promise an assurance of complete and permanent cleansing? It does because God creates within us *new hearts*. In this story, the woman believed that this person, Jesus, could do what no other person could. It was enough for her to touch even His clothes to be healed. So with amazing courage she penetrated the crowds and touched the robe of Jesus. The story goes on to say, "Immediately her bleeding stopped and she felt in her body that she was freed from her suffering. At once Jesus realized that power had gone out from him. He turned around in the crowd and asked, 'Who touched my clothes?'" (Mark 5:29-30).

Why did Jesus stop and ask this question, "Who touched my clothes?" There were people all around Him bumping into Him. The important thing is not geographical proximity to Jesus. What matters is faith and intimacy. Furthermore, why did Jesus embarrass this woman by exposing her in public? Jesus wanted to publicly give her the assurance of healing not only of her bleeding problem but also of her heart. The story concludes,

"You see the people crowding against you," his disciples answered, "and yet you can ask, 'Who touched me?'"

But Jesus kept looking around to see who had done it. Then the woman, knowing what had happened to her, came and fell at his feet and, trembling with fear, told him the whole truth. He said to her, "Daughter, your faith has healed you. Go in peace and be freed from your suffering." (verses 31-34)

I could have stopped at that point. People's hearts were moved in a deep way as the two stories touched their felt needs at the deepest level. But I had more time, so I continued with the third story.

## THE THIRD STORY

I reminded the villagers that Jesus was on His way to the town where Jairus lived to heal his twelve-year-old daughter. But He had been interrupted by this woman and her need. So I asked them, "How would you feel if you were in the place of this desperate man?" Jairus must have been struggling with anxiety, and his heart must have dropped down in despair when one of his servants came to him with the message that it was too late; his daughter had died. Jesus turned to Jairus, the synagogue leader, and told him, "Don't be afraid; just believe" (Mark 5:36).

Upon reaching the home of Jairus, Jesus went into the room where the dead girl lay and asked everyone to get out of the room, except for the father, the mother, and a few disciples. Then "he took her by the hand and said to her, '*Talitha koum!*' (which means, 'Little girl, I say to you, get up!'). Immediately the girl stood up and walked around (she was twelve years old). At this they were completely astonished. He . . . told them to give her something to eat" (verses 41-43).

Muslims, and especially those who adhere to folk Islam, are terrified by death and the dying process. There is a well-known book among Muslims, written in Arabic, with the title *Torture of the Grave*. Fear of the unknown and uncertainty about what is behind the "door" bring about a great deal of anxiety. According to Bill Musk in his book *The Unseen Face of Islam*, death is believed to be a separation of the soul from the body. Two angels are appointed to interrogate the person who dies: *Naker* and *Munkar*. Preparing for death sometimes takes a lifetime. When the head of a family is dying, the family brings a practitioner to chant the Qur'an in the room of the dying person. They burn incense and observe certain restrictions about who should be allowed to visit the dying man. A small Qur'an is placed under his pillow and, if possible, a few drops of holy Zamzam water are sprayed on his face.* The relatives of the dying man yearn that he might die on a Friday while lying on his right side, the more honorable side.**

The forty villagers who were listening to this final story in Mark chapter 5 had that background of Muslim beliefs, and they were gripped by Jesus and His power even to raise that little girl from the dead. As soon as I finished my presentation, there was a question-answer time. The first question was asked by one of the women. Politely she raised her index finger and made a statement followed by a question: "I want to believe in Jesus. How do I do it?" I almost fell out of my chair. I had not expected a question like that to be asked in public. Most likely her husband was sitting on the other side of the room.

## SOME PRINCIPLES

In these last two chapters, we looked at paradigms. Here are a few principles:

1. There are several paradigms in the Bible. We Christians, especially in the West, tend to assume that the guilt/righteousness paradigm is the only one. In reality, there are other paradigms, such as shame/honor, defilement/clean, and fear/power. These three other paradigms are very important to Muslims. Of course, there are even more paradigms, and people who have a heart for postmodern people, for example, need to figure out what their paradigm is.

---

\* When pilgrims return home after the pilgrimage, or the Hajj, they bring with them water from the well of Zamzam in Mecca for medicinal purposes and for blessings.

\** Friday is the most blessed day of the week. The right hand is for eating and greeting people. The left hand is for ignoble use.

2. My friend Waldron Scott, who is a longtime missionary, and I interacted over the power of paradigms. He wrote,

The guilt/righteousness paradigm has become a central paradigm to Protestant Christianity. It did not formally appear in Christian theology until the Reformers (sixteenth century)—three-fourths of the way through Christian history. The prevailing paradigm before that was St. Anselm's (eleventh century) satisfaction paradigm, which is based on the shame/honor paradigm. It prevailed within Christianity for five centuries—equal to the Reformer's paradigm. Before either the Reformers or Anselm, there was the classical paradigm, which prevailed for a thousand years and is based on the fear/power paradigm and is still widely held today. I do not know whether the defilement/clean paradigm has ever been utilized in Christian history as the basis for a major paradigm of the Atonement.[1]

3. We need to learn to present the gospel with all four paradigms, but we need always to *start* with the paradigm of the person we are connecting with.

4. As I listened to a lecture on postmodernity, I was struck by how much I can learn to connect with Muslims if I dare to come out of my traditional approach in my evangelism. The contrasts between modernity and postmodernity reminded me so much of the differences between the legal paradigm and the other paradigms. The contrasts between modernity and postmodernity parallel the various approaches used by Christians in their outreach to Muslims:

Modernism . . . leans heavily upon rationalism and material proofs in determining reality. In contrast the postmodern mind is no longer satisfied with evidence in answering its deepest questions. The heart and the emotions are now taking over. . . . Whereas the modern worldview tends toward optimism or eventual progress as humankind learns to conquer its environment, the postmodern is more pessimistic or fatalistic in its view of history. The postmodern is wary of science and thinks that it causes more problems for humanity than good. Moderns tended to believe in absolutes, universals, and objective truth claims. The postmodern shrugs at all this and operates as if belief is relative, truth is more created and therefore, subjective. The modern's emphasis on the autonomous individual focused on conquest runs smack dab against the postmodern's emphasis on community, focused on cooperation. Modernity's concern with purpose, design and hierarchical order stifles postmodernity's penchant for play and chance (chaos) in a world where everyone is an equal participant and gives input. The postmodern loves to engage the heart above the head, can actually go above the natural world to entertain the supernatural, and lives for a world that stresses diversity more than unified subjugation.[2]

5. The good news of the gospel addresses the deep felt needs of all humans.

   a. To those with a guilt/righteousness paradigm, the good news is that we can be completely forgiven because of what Christ accomplished on the cross. He gave us His righteousness and took upon Himself our sin — past, present, and future.*

---

\* Two chapters in my book *Unshackled and Growing* address this topic.

b. To those with a shame/honor paradigm, Christ covered the shame of our nakedness by wrapping us from our heads to our toes with His robe of righteousness (see Isaiah 61:10).

c. To those with a defilement/clean paradigm, Christ confronted the Jews for focusing on outward cleansing rather than their need for having new hearts (see Mark 7:20-23). Christ creates within us clean and new hearts (see Ezekiel 36:26).

d. To those with a fear/power paradigm, in the huge cosmic battle, Christ crushed Satan by taking his strongest weapon—fear of death—and transforming death into a gate that leads into eternal life.*

## Questions for Reflection and Discussion

1. Go back to the beginning of the chapter. Is Ahmad justified in his statement? What do you think of the statement made by the Nigerian Christian?
2. What are some biblical passages that address other paradigms besides the familiar guilt/righteousness paradigm?
3. What components do you think make up the paradigm of postmoderns? What themes from the Bible address these?
4. In Western countries like the United States, New Zealand, and England, how much would a student struggle with guilt after cheating on an exam? Would it be more painful if he got caught? What does that tell us about the guilt/righteousness paradigm in the West?

---

* In *Unshackled and Growing*, I have a whole chapter on this paradigm.

# CHAPTER 12

# SIMILARITIES AND DIFFERENCES

*What a difference between the Bible and the Qur'an and between Jesus and Muhammad! Why are the Muslims so blind to the facts when it is so obvious?*

— AN ARGENTINEAN CHRISTIAN

In his presentation, Ahmad said, *"You start with wrong assumptions by comparing our prophet Muhammad to Christ and comparing the Qur'an to the Bible. You think that you have figured us out and understand our theology. I am sorry to say you have a skewed understanding of our religion."*

Years ago I went to an American city to visit an acquaintance who was prejudiced against Muslims. As soon as I reached his house, he started sharing with me his excitement about a book he was reading—a book about Islam written by an evangelical American. The things he read confirmed his prejudiced conclusions about Islam. What amazed him, though, was a paragraph in which the author claimed that the Qur'an taught that only white people will go to heaven, while blacks will go to hell. That amazed me, too, so I asked him to show me the book and that particular paragraph.

When I read it, I was shocked by the way the author asserted his conclusion about the Qur'an. I was glad, though, that he had included a reference from the Qur'an at the end of that paragraph. I assured my host that from what I know about the Qur'an, God favors the pious believer irrespective of race and color. I also promised him that I would check that passage in the Qur'an and get back to him. When I did check that verse, in both Arabic and English, I found out that the author had totally misinterpreted it. It says, "One day some faces will turn white while other faces will turn black. Those whose faces are blackened [will be asked]: 'Did you disbelieve after your [profession of] faith? Taste torment because you have disbelieved!'" (Surah 3:106). The passage was talking about the righteous and how their faces will be "whitened" on the Day of Judgment. In contrast, the evil will have their faces, as it were, "blackened" and shamed. The Qur'an was not talking about racial preferences but about being shamed or honored on the Day of Judgment.

How many people have read that book without checking the verse quoted from the Qur'an? How far has the rumor about the claimed prejudice of the Qur'an against blacks spread? How many Christians' prejudice was reinforced by that book?

One of the quickest ways for me to evaluate a book written about Islam by a Christian is to try to find out what is in the mind of the author. What comparisons is he or she making between Islam and Christianity? If the underlying assumptions that the author makes in his or her book are comparisons between Christ and Muhammad, and the Bible and the Qur'an, then I know that the book is not worth reading. It will end up with skewed conclusions. It will not be only a waste of time to read but will also result in great confusion in the mind of the reader.*

## COMPARISONS AND CONTRASTS

As we explore the ways elements of Christianity and Islam have been compared, it will help to look at a piece of history. The first theological controversy in Islam took place shortly after the death of Muhammad and was championed by the *Mu'tazila* sect. They claimed that God existed from eternity, while the Qur'an, God's Word, had a starting point. In other words, the Qur'an was not eternal and was created. It began when Muhammad started receiving the revelation through the angel Gabriel. Mainstream theologians, on the other hand, strongly disagreed with the Mu'tazila scholars and declared them heretics. Those mainstream theologians argued that since God is eternal, His Word is eternal. God cannot exist as a silent God; therefore, His Word is eternal and uncreated. In their understanding of the Qur'an, they came to a conclusion very close to, but not identical with, what we believe about Christ.

With what or whom should the Qur'an be compared?

In our Christian theology, one of the main texts on Christology in the New Testament is found at the beginning of the gospel of John: "In the beginning was the Word [*Logos*], and the Word [Logos] was with God, and the Word [Logos] was God. He [the Logos] was with God in the beginning" (1:1-2). The eternal, uncreated Word of God (the Logos), who existed with God from eternity, visited earth and was incarnated. We know Him as Jesus Christ. In another text on Christology in the New Testament, we see more about Jesus:

---

\* At the end of this book I have included a list of recommended books.

He is the image of the invisible God. . . . For by him all things were created: things in heaven and on earth, visible and invisible, whether thrones or powers or rulers or authorities; all things were created by him and for him. He is before all things, and in him all things hold together. . . . For God was pleased to have all his fullness dwell in him, and through him to reconcile to himself all things, whether things on earth or things in heaven, by making peace through his blood, shed on the cross. (Colossians 1:15-17,19-20)

From these two texts and others in the New Testament, we learn a great deal about the Logos, the eternal, uncreated Word of God—His incarnation, His living on earth with perfect righteousness that fully satisfied the absolute demands of God, His crucifixion, His resurrection, and His ascension. In a similar way, Muslims believe that the Qur'an is the eternal and uncreated Word of God. In contrast, though, the Word of God was incarnated in the form of the contents of a book that *revealed God's will rather than His person*. So the comparison between Christ and the Qur'an is there and it is real, but it *falls short*. Who would Muhammad compare to in our biblical theology?

According to Islamic theology, Muhammad never learned to read and write. From AD 612 on, he started receiving revelations from God through the angel Gabriel. The contents of what he received came from the Book in heaven (Al Lawh al Mahfouz). Because Muhammad was illiterate, what he received a few verses at a time from 610 to 632 was 100 percent accurate. With his photographic memory, he would memorize what he received and then dictate it to those who were literate. According to Muslim historians, twenty years after his death (in 652), the Qur'an was canonized.

Muslims with orthodox theology believe that Muhammad did not do any miracles, such as healings. Yet he experienced the biggest miracle in history. Although he was illiterate, he received the eternal and uncreated Word of God, the Qur'an. How could an illiterate person come up with a book like the Qur'an? Muslims believe that the way Muhammad received the Qur'an was unique and miraculous and no other person on earth could repeat the experience. (Muslims refer to *'Ijaz Al Qur'an*, which means the miraculous nature of the Qur'an.)

The person in our Bible who would most resemble Muhammad is Mary. She was a virgin, and yet through the miraculous intervention of God, she became pregnant with the Logos, the eternal, uncreated Word of God. From what we see in the New Testament, she did not do any miracles, yet she experienced the biggest miracle in history. She miraculously became pregnant and gave birth to God incarnate, the Lord Jesus Christ. How we see Mary is how Muslims see Muhammad. The virginity of Mary is exactly like the illiteracy of Muhammad. If Mary had three children and then got pregnant, who would believe that her conception of the fourth child was miraculous? If Muhammad was literate and had previously written three books and then came up with the fourth book, the Qur'an, who would believe that it was any different from the other books he had written?

It is interesting to observe that as Mary has been venerated in our Christian history, Muhammad has been venerated in the Islamic history as well.

## The Issue of Inspiration

Ahmad said, "The Qur'an was not written by men. It was dictated by God through an angel. Why should I leave my superior message and replace it with an inferior message that relies on a less reliable book?"

We stated earlier that Muslims believe that parts of the Book in heaven were given to Moses and David, and other parts were given to

Jesus. Moses, David, and Jesus knew how to read and write.* Muslims also believe that Moses and David wrote what they received in their own words; therefore, there was room for human error. Likewise, the followers of Christ wrote what they received from Jesus in their own words, and again there was room for human error. In contrast, Muslims believe that since Muhammad did not know how to read and write, what he received was a photocopy of the Book in heaven. The Qur'an, they believe, had its source in heaven, and the very words are the words of God with no human intervention.

Muslims see our Bible as they see their tradition (Hadith). The life and teachings of Muhammad were written by Muslims who loved God. Their writings were superior to other books because they had to do with the life and teachings of their great prophet Muhammad. But since the authors were human, their writings had the potential for human error. On this basis, Muslims believe that some elements of the Hadith were reliable and others were unreliable. This is how they see the writers of the Gospels and the rest of our Bible. On the other hand, they see the Qur'an exactly as we see the Ten Commandments—delivered directly from God—and therefore they see the Qur'an as superior to the Bible. The question for them, then, is why they should leave their superior message and replace it with an inferior message that relies on a less reliable book.

Muslims have a great challenge to meet, however. If there are grammatical, geographical, or historical mistakes in the Qur'an, whose mistakes are they? They cannot be the mistakes of Muhammad; they have to be the mistakes of God because Muhammad while receiving the revelation was merely a tape recorder. Some scholars agree that there are mistakes in the Qur'an. The Qur'an has not yet received the scrutiny

---

* Some very uninformed Muslims may still believe that Jesus wrote the New Testament. The majority of Muslims believe that Jesus received the New Testament from God and passed it to His disciples, who then wrote it down.

that the Bible has gone through by Christian theologians like Rudolf Bultmann and others. Will the Qur'an be allowed to go through similar scrutiny? If so, will it pass the test?

In regard to the Bible, throughout history there have been several theories addressing biblical inspiration:

1. Some scholars consider inspiration to mean nothing more than *enlightenment*. Those who wrote the various books of the Bible were inspired or enlightened when they wrote them. Shakespeare was similarly inspired when he wrote *Macbeth*. When people read *Macbeth*, they sense that it is superior to other literature. The proof of its inspiration is the fact that it continues to be studied by students around the world. Similarly, the proof of the inspiration of the Bible is its continued impact on the lives of people throughout history and around the world.

2. Another theory of inspiration states that the *ideas originally came from God*. The writers provided the rest — the stories, thoughts, and words. So according to people who believe in this theory, the book of Jonah, for instance, is the product of the writer who made up the story of a man named Jonah and his experience with a big fish and the people of Nineveh. What came from God was only the essence of the story, which had to do with the ethnocentricity of the people of God in contrast to God's mercy on the nations.

3. Another theory states that the *thoughts were inspired by God, but not the words*. So the writers of the books of the Bible received the thoughts from God and then wrote those thoughts in their own words. My difficulty with this theory lies in the fact that I cannot come up with a thought without words. The way I see it is that a thought is not a thought

unless it is conceived and expressed through words.

4. The theory that most Christians adhere to rests on the fact that inspiration "never had its origin in the will of man, but men spoke from God as they were carried along by the Holy Spirit" (2 Peter 1:21). God inspired not only the *ideas* but the *thoughts* and *words* as well. Isaiah's Hebrew language was superior to the Hebrew language that Amos had. God did not need to teach Amos better Hebrew to give him His perfect message. Out of the limited vocabulary that Amos had, the Holy Spirit chose the very words that were adequate vehicles to give us His full and perfect message.

Furthermore, God did not need to give Amos broader education to make him adequate to receive God's revelation. The writers of the Bible were not passive instruments who were manipulated by God so that He could protect His message from corruption. The Bible writers' limited education and knowledge (believing, for example, that the sun revolved around the earth) did not deprive us from receiving God's perfect message. *The Holy Spirit* was also very much *involved in the canonization process* of the whole Bible. Out of the hundreds of manuscripts considered and scrutinized for years, only thirty-nine books were accepted into the Old Testament and only twenty-seven became part of the New Testament. *The Holy Spirit* was involved in the *selection and elimination process.*

5. A few scholars in our Christian history have believed in a theory called *mechanical inspiration.* These people believe that the whole Bible was dictated by God to the writers of the Bible. Just as the Ten Commandments were inscribed by God, the whole Bible was dictated, word for word, by God. People who believe in this theory have a hard time making

sense of Bible passages that assume, for example, that our earth is the center of our solar system. According to this theory, these errors are not the errors of man but the mistakes of God. If most Christians believed in the theory of mechanical inspiration, the Bible could not have gone through scholarly higher criticism and come out intact.

Muslims have a huge challenge facing them regarding the Qur'an and their belief in mechanical inspiration. So far they have escaped the scrutiny that the Bible went through. But with the age of the Internet and globalization, it will not be long before Muslims themselves begin to scrutinize the Qur'an.

As I listened to my friend Ahmad say, "The Qur'an was not written by men. It was dictated by God through an angel," I thought that there is a time and a place to challenge him. Now is not the right time.

## QUESTIONS FOR REFLECTION AND DISCUSSION

1. Go back to the beginning of the chapter. What do you think of Ahmad's statement? What does the statement made by the Argentinean Christian reveal about him?
2. In what ways are the Qur'an (the way Muslims see it) and Jesus (the way we see Him) similar and different? How would you compare Mary to Muhammad?
3. What does the Bible say about the reliability of the Bible in 2 Peter 1:16-21?

We did not follow cleverly invented stories when we told you about the power and coming of our Lord Jesus Christ, but we were eyewitnesses of his majesty. [What is Peter referring to? Who were the eyewitnesses?] For he received honor and glory from God the Father when the voice came to him from the Majestic Glory, saying, "This is my Son, whom I love; with him I am well pleased." We ourselves heard this voice that came from heaven when we were with him on the sacred mountain. [Peter is referring to the experience that he, John, and James had when they saw Jesus transfigured. Did Peter have doubts about that experience? Even if he had doubts, he could have gone to John or James and asked each of them separately to describe in detail what they experienced on the mountain.]

And we have the word of the prophets made more certain [Other translations say "more dependable." In other words, Peter is saying that the Word of God is even more dependable than the experience that he, John, and James had], and you will do well to pay attention to it, as to a light shining in a dark place, until the day dawns and the morning star rises in your hearts. Above all, you must understand that no prophecy of Scripture came about by the prophet's own interpretation. For prophecy never had its origin in the will of man, but men spoke from God as they were carried along by the Holy Spirit.

4. If you were a Muslim, what difficulties would you face in having to believe in the mechanical inspiration of the Qur'an?

CHAPTER 13

# THE BIBLE AND
# THE QUR'AN

*We in the Western world have a Judeo-Christian culture,*
*so of course the Jews are closer to us than the Muslims.*
— AN AUSTRALIAN CHRISTIAN

In describing the Muslim worldview, Ahmad said,

> Jews today do not recognize Jesus as the Messiah. Their high
> priest, two thousand years ago, declared Him a blasphemer,
> and I think you believe that the Jews, along with the Romans,
> killed Jesus. On the other hand, we Muslims highly respect
> Him. We believe that Jesus was born of a virgin, healed the
> blind and those with leprosy, raised the dead, is now with God
> in heaven, and will come back on the Day of Judgment as the
> Sign of the Hour. Why do you feel theologically closer to the
> Jews than to the Muslims? I am not saying culturally; I am

saying theologically. Of course you feel much closer culturally to the Jews than to us, the Muslims, because many Jews
have a European background and many are citizens of the
U.S. Again, my question is this: Why do you feel theologically
closer to the Jews than to the Muslims?

In a private conversation with Ahmad, he shared with me his
dismay and his inability to understand why Christians in the West
assume that Jews are theologically closer to them than Muslims are.
He wanted to discuss in detail our understanding of the term *Judeo-
Christian morality*. He questioned whether Jews and Christians have
the same moral standards. He shared with me his understanding that
the Jews believe in the principle of an eye for an eye and a tooth for a
tooth. In contrast, Christians believe in the teaching of Jesus regarding loving their enemies and forgiving those who sin against them. If
that is the case, he asked me, then how can Jews and Christians have
the same "Judeo-Christian morality"? He concluded that Jews and
Muslims are alike in their morality of an eye for an eye and a tooth for
a tooth and are both very different from Christians. I partially agreed
with his conclusion.

The *Judeo-Christian* term, as it is traditionally understood in the
West, is often misunderstood. In my judgment, it should refer only to
Christians who believe in the Old Testament and the New Testament
and read the Old Testament in light of the New Testament. The morality of these Christians is based on the ancient Jewish yearning for the
coming of the Messiah, which, Christians believe, was fulfilled in the
person of Jesus Christ.

Jews, on the other hand, do not believe that Jesus Christ is their
awaited Messiah. As my friend Ahmad said, Caiaphas, the high priest
two thousand years ago, declared Jesus a blasphemer. The Jews' morality is based on the Old Testament and on their commentaries that
interpret the Old Testament in light of the fact that they are still

waiting for the Messiah. Therefore the *Judeo-Christian* term used on a purely theological basis does not apply to Jews since they do not recognize Jesus or the New Testament. It applies only to Christians. My friend Waldron Scott pointed out that Jews over the past century, as they have lived in the West, have accepted Western Christian morality and civilization and aligned themselves with it. In that respect, we can speak of a Judeo-Christian culture.

The morality of Christians is based on three things:

1. The absolute will of God as revealed in the Ten Commandments
2. The example and teachings of Jesus
3. The new life in the Spirit

Christians used all three to form Western civilization, and modern Jews have "bought into" Western civilization. Jews do not embrace Jesus as the Messiah, but they have in modern times embraced Western culture in general, which both Christians and Jews understand has a biblical basis in both the Old and New Testaments.

As I continued my discussion with Ahmad, he repeatedly asked me why Christians believe we are *theologically* closer to the Jews than to the Muslims. This was one of his burning issues. For us to get into this topic through the exchange of e-mails, we had to look at passages in both the Qur'an and the Bible. I find the books of John Gilchrist to be very helpful in getting background facts and information about the Qur'an.[1]

## BIBLE CHARACTERS IN THE QUR'AN

The Qur'an teaches about the prophets and messengers sent as warners to lead humanity to faith in the one God. It recognizes many of the prophets and patriarchs in the Bible. Muslims are commanded to believe in all the prophets without making distinctions. The Qur'an identifies the following as prophets: Adam, Abraham, Isaac, Ishmael, Jacob, and Moses. The list does not include Isaiah, Jeremiah, and Ezekiel. Also omitted or glossed over is the sacrificial system that exists in the Scriptures.

The New Testament figures that appear in the Qur'an are Isa (Jesus), Mariam (Mary), Yahya (John the Baptist), and Zakariya (the father of John the Baptist). Mary has a special place in the Qur'an. Not only was she the mother of Jesus, but it is believed that she was a virgin and that she was not touched by Satan.* The only other person who was not touched by Satan at birth was Jesus. The Qur'an says about Mary and Jesus, "And she who guarded her chastity, so We breathed some of Our spirit into her, and set both her and her son up as a sign for [everyone in] the Universe" (Surah 21:91).

## JESUS

Jesus has several titles in the Qur'an. He is *Al Masih* (the Christ). He is also called *Kalimatuhu* (His Word) and *Ruhon minhu* (a spirit from Him). Muslims believe that Jesus was born of a virgin, healed the blind and lepers, and raised the dead. The Qur'an also teaches that Christ as a boy performed a miracle when He created birds of clay figures

---

* According to Muslim tradition (Hadith), every baby at birth gets touched by Satan during the birth process, and that is the reason babies cry right after their birth. This comes close to, but is not exactly, what we believe in the doctrine of original sin. Only two exceptions to this rule exist in Islam: Jesus and Mary. They were the only two individuals who were not touched by Satan during their birth. Al-Bukhari attested to that. Muhammad was touched by Satan during his birth. How does folk Islam deal with this issue? Muslim tradition points out a critical event that took place during the boyhood of Muhammad. When he was playing with other boys in the courtyard of his foster mother, he had a fit and fell on the floor. Muslims believe that an angel came and opened his chest and his heart and took out a black clot that was inside his heart. That clot was symbolic of sin, or the weakness that comes as a result of being touched by Satan during birth. He was cleansed from that weakness by the angel.

(see Surah 5:110). The Qur'an teaches that Jesus was taken to heaven (see Surah 4:158) and that He will return to earth at the end of time called the Sign of the Hour (see Surah 43:61).

On the other hand, Islam differs from the Bible on central issues. According to the traditional interpretation of the Qur'an, Jesus was not crucified. Furthermore the text of this denial is in the context of the Jews and their disbelief. This text speaks of

> their [the Jews'] breaking the charter, their disbelief in God's signs, their killing the prophets without any right to do so . . . their disbelief and their talking such terrible slander about Mary. . . . They neither killed nor crucified him, even though it seemed so to them. Those who disagree about it are in doubt concerning it; they have no [real] knowledge about it except by following conjecture. No one is certain they killed him! Rather God lifted him up towards Himself. God is Powerful, Wise!" (Surah 4:155-158)

For Muslims, to believe that the Jews succeeded in crucifying Jesus would be to believe that Jesus and God were defeated. So they believe that God intervened miraculously and took Jesus up to Himself and that someone else was placed on the cross. It appeared to the Jews that it was Jesus, but in reality it was someone else. Some of them believe it was Judas.

Another major difference between Christian and Muslim theologies regarding Jesus has to do with His deity. The Qur'an asserts, "Christians say: 'Christ was God's son.' That is what they say with their mouths, imitating what those have said who disbelieved before them. May God fight them off for what they have trumped up!" (Surah 9:30).

According to Muslim historians, Muhammad as a young man

visited Damascus with the caravans that belonged to Khadijah, his future wife. During his visit, Muhammad must have seen churches in that city, and if he went into any of those churches, he would have seen a huge statue of a woman carrying a baby. If he asked about the woman and the baby, he would have been told that it was Mary, the mother of God, and Jesus, the son of God. His conclusion would have been that Christians are getting into *shirk*, or ascribing partners to God. This was considered in the Qur'an to be the greatest sin and the only unforgivable sin. How could God have a physical relationship with a woman and have a son? On this basis, the deity of Christ and the Triune God were rejected in the Qur'an.

## THE BIBLE

In the Qur'an, the Christians and the Jews were distinguished from the pagans and the idolaters. The Qur'an refers to both as the people of the Book. They are criticized in the Qur'an as having deviated from the teaching of their Scriptures: "Let the people of the Gospel judge by what God has sent down in it; Those who do not judge by what God has sent down are perverse!" (Surah 5:47). And "SAY: 'People of the Book, you will not make any point until you keep up the Torah and the Gospel, as well as anything that has been sent down to you by your Lord'" (Surah 5:68).

Muhammad believed that the Old Testament and the New Testament were in full harmony with the Qur'an. At that time in his life, he believed that the Qur'an was simply an Arabic equivalent to the former books. The Injil (the Gospel) had been delivered to Jesus (see Surah 57:27). The Tawrat and Zabour (the Torah and the Psalms — i.e., the Old Testament) were sent to the Jews (see Surah 4:136; 5:47). The Qur'an was sent to Muhammad partly to confirm former revelation and in the Arabic language because the Arabs had no book of their own and no prophet of their own and nothing in their own language. The Qur'an was sent to the Arabs in a tailored form primarily for the purpose of completing what was missing in previous revelations.

According to Surah 3:78, a group of the people in the Qur'an, the Jews and the Christians, were not accused of tampering with the text of the Bible but only of "twisting their tongues" (Surah 2:101; 4:46; 5:44; 2:75). What does that mean? "A group of them twist their tongues around concerning the Book so you will reckon [something] comes from the Book while it is not from the Book. They say: 'It comes from God!' while it is not from God. They knowingly tell a lie about God!" (Surah 3:78).

Some modern Muslims today interpret this verse to mean that the Bible was twisted because of a motivation to build the church. They say Christians would "twist their tongues" and tell lies about God because they wanted to control the masses. According to Muslims, the Council of Nicea was an example of this. I personally find this interpretation to be a weak argument that cannot be defended by Muslims.

Then what does "twisting their tongues" really mean? Let me illustrate with this incident. I was sitting with a group of young, single Christian men after they finished their Bible study discussion. I wanted to joke with them, so I asked them if they had memorized Proverbs 32:15. In the book of Proverbs, there are only thirty-one chapters, with chapter 31 being a famous chapter about the godly woman. None of the men remembered this. So I quoted the "verse" to them: "A man without his wife is like a kitchen without a knife." I tried to keep a straight face as long as possible and then told them that I made it up. Then I told them how my younger son made up the next verse in that imaginary chapter, Proverbs 32:16: "A father without his sons is like a cowboy without his guns." We all laughed, especially about "verse 16."

I can imagine Muhammad in the city of Medina coming to some of

the Jewish leaders with excitement about how God was giving him revelation from the Book in heaven. Perhaps Muhammad expected those
Jewish leaders to be equally excited with him that God had not for-
saken the Arabs. Instead, perhaps, they made up "verses" that rhymed
like the ones my son and I made up, and for a moment he believed
them because what they quoted rhymed, until they started laughing at
him. I think an incident like this was the background for the text in
the Qur'an that talks about the twisting of their tongues.

## THE PEOPLE OF THE BOOK

Muhammad had no doubts about the Old Testament and the New
Testament. According to the Qur'an, the Injil and the Tawrat were
the actual Scriptures the Jews and the Christians had at the time of
Muhammad (see Surah 5:46; 5:50; 7:157).

As for the people of the Book, the Jews and the Christians, a group
of them will be accepted on the Day of Judgment. The rest are regarded
as having deviated from following their own Scriptures, turned away
from God, and become opponents of Muhammad. Collectively, they
are ridiculed for their claims to have a monopoly over the truth, even
over and against each other: "Jews say: 'Christians have no point to
make;' while Christians say: 'The Jews have no point to make.' Yet they
(all) quote from the [same] Book. Likewise those who do not know
anything make a statement similar to theirs. God will judge between
them on Resurrection Day concerning how they have been differing"
(Surah 2:113).

## THE JEWS AND THE CHRISTIANS

According to some parts of the Qur'an, the Jews are the fiercest enemies of Islam (see Surah 5:44; 5:67; 2:96; 5:84). Also, we read, "You

will find the most violently hostile people towards those who believe [the Muslims] are the Jews and those who associate [others with God]" (Surah 5:82). "Abraham was neither a Jew nor a Christian, but he was a Seeker [after Truth], a Muslim" (Surah 3:67). Abraham believed that God existed and that he was One. He believed in God before the existence of Judaism and Christianity. In essence, Abraham was a "Muslim" since Islam means submission to the one God.

The Christians, on the other hand, are spoken of with more favor: "You will find the most affectionate of them towards those who believe [the Muslims], are those who say: 'We are Christians.' That is because some of them are priests and monks; they do not behave so proudly" (Surah 5:82). Christians are rebuked as well, though: "They have adopted their scholars and monks as lords instead of God, plus Christ, the son of Mary. Yet they have been ordered to serve only God Alone; there is no deity except Him. Glory be to Him ahead of whatever they may associate [with Him]!" (Surah 9:31).

According to some Christian scholars, close to the end of the life of Muhammad, the Muslim armies clashed with the Christian armies north of Arabia, and so Muhammad's attitude toward Christians became hostile: "You who believe, do not accept Jews or Christians as sponsors; some of them act as sponsors for one another. Any of you who makes friends with them becomes one of them. God does not guide such wrongdoing folk" (Surah 5:51). "Fight the ones among those who were given the Book who do not believe in God nor the Last Day, nor forbid whatever God and His messenger have forbidden, nor profess the True Religion, until they pay the polltax of their own accord and act submissive" (Surah 9:29).

## COMING BACK

Coming back to where we started in this chapter, Ahmad made a bold statement and then asked me a disturbing question:

191

We believe that Jesus was born of a virgin, healed the blind and those with leprosy, raised the dead, is now with God in heaven, and will come back on the Day of Judgment as the Sign of the Hour. Why do you feel theologically closer to the Jews than to the Muslims?

Why do we feel theologically closer to the Jews than to the Muslims? There could be various reasons for that. Partly, it is because of our eschatology (our theology of the end times).* Another major reason is that Christians believe that the Old Testament is part of God's revelation, and they are suspicious regarding the origin of the Qur'an. Still another reason could be the huge cultural gap that exists between Christians and Muslims. Western Christians feel closer to Jews than to Muslims because Jews have lived in the West for two millennia, whereas Muslims invaded Europe on two major occasions, and Christendom fought successive wars against Muslims (the Crusades). This is the case despite the fact that Western Christendom has not always had close relations with Jews; on the contrary, Jews have been ostracized and persecuted within Christendom from time to time. It is only with the Enlightenment and the emergence of democratic ideals and increasingly pluralistic societies that we felt the need to speak of a common Judeo-Christian tradition. To add to all this, the confusing politics in the Middle East do not help our relations with Muslims.

Most of these factors deal not with theology but with culture. So the challenge that Ahmad presented still holds: "I am not saying culturally; I am saying theologically. Of course you feel much closer culturally to the Jews than to us, the Muslims. My question is this: Why do you feel theologically closer to the Jews than to the Muslims?" If you examine the theology rather than the cultural factors, how would you respond to Ahmad's question? Do you feel theologically closer to

---

* There is a chapter on eschatology in the addendum.

the Jews than to the Muslims? If so, what are your reasons?

In this section we tried to unpack and address issues that Ahmad raised about our message and about us, the messengers. In the next section we will try to unpack and address issues raised about him, the receiver.

## QUESTIONS FOR REFLECTION AND DISCUSSION

1. Go back to the beginning of the chapter. How do you respond to Ahmad's question, "Why do you feel theologically closer to the Jews than to the Muslims?"
2. What are your impressions of Judeo-Christian morality and tradition?
3. Do you think Muslims in general would think this chapter is accurate in its description of what the Qur'an teaches? In what ways might they be critical?
4. Do you think Christians in the West would agree that this chapter is accurate in its description of what the Qur'an teaches? In what ways might they be critical?
5. Why is there a polarization in perceptions of Islam between Christians and Muslims? What factors contribute to this polarization?

# PART THREE

# THE RECEIVER

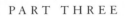

### CONNECTING
### WITH MUSLIMS

CHAPTER 14

# RELATIONAL EVANGELISM

*Muslims who become Christians need to pay the cost of following Christ and should not develop dependency on us, the Christians. God will provide for their needs.*

— A FRENCH CHRISTIAN

In response to American Christians who tried to convert him, Ahmad wrote, *"If I converted to Christianity, my support system in life would be completely demolished. I would become, as it were, homeless and without family. How would I live? Are you able to provide for me a completely new support system?"*

Paul, in his letter to Titus, gave advice on how to care for his church. In 2:4-5 he advised Titus what to teach older women and what they in turn should teach younger women. Paul wrote about the older women, "Then they can train the younger women to love their husbands and children, to be self-controlled and pure, to be busy at home, to be kind, and to be subject to their husbands, so that no one will malign the word of God." The word *malign* is a difficult word in English. It means treating something—in this case, the Word of God—with disrespect or contempt.

Here is the list of what older women should teach younger women. There are seven commands:

1. Love their husbands.
2. Love their children.
3. Be self-controlled.
4. Be pure.
5. Be busy at home. In other words, young wives should take care of their domestic responsibilities. (In those days, the roles of the husbands and wives were more defined. The husband earned the money, and the wife took care of the domestic responsibilities.)
6. Be kind.
7. Be subject to their husbands.*

What surprises me in this list is the absence of a command to evangelize. What if the husband of this young wife is not a believer in Christ? Shouldn't she share with him the gospel? Shouldn't she proclaim to him the truth of the plan of salvation? Paul expected himself to evangelize. He said, "Yet when I preach the gospel, I cannot boast, for I am compelled to preach. Woe to me if I do not preach the gospel!" (1 Corinthians 9:16). In his advice to Timothy, Paul wrote, "Preach the

---

* Submission is often confused with subservience, or being like a "doormat." Yet submission is very different from subservience. Jesus was submissive, and Paul was submissive, but both were very far from being subservient. Submission has its roots in believing that God is in sovereign control of our circumstances and that no one else determines our destiny.

Word; be prepared in season and out of season" (2 Timothy 4:2). Paul and Timothy were mature Christians, and it was expected of them that they should proclaim the truth of the gospel. In contrast, nowhere in the letters of Paul do we see him asking young Christians to proclaim the message of the gospel. Why is it that young wives in Titus 2:4-5 were not commanded to proclaim the message of salvation?

## SCENARIOS ON MARRIAGE

I will create here two fictional situations that are in reality *composites* of the situations of *real people* I have known in Egypt or in other parts of the world where I have lived. These two scenarios are developed in light of Titus 2:4-5. The first scenario describes a violation of this passage, and the second scenario demonstrates what happens when the commands in Titus 2:4-5 are put into practice.

### THE FIRST SCENARIO

Let us imagine a young woman who six months ago married a middle-class man in a third world country. Both she and her husband came from a nominal Christian background, and neither had a personal relationship with the Lord. This young lady grew up as an only child in a relatively rich family who spoiled and pampered her. She never learned to cook or keep her room tidy or carry out any domestic responsibilities. Her college studies were all she cared about.

After she got married, she slept in every morning till about nine, and the rest of the day she lived an idle lifestyle. She did not have a job and was not motivated to look for one. Her husband, on the other hand, woke up every morning at six and went to work an hour later. He returned home from work every day at about five thirty. This husband tolerated his wife's self-centered lifestyle and ate sandwiches for his meals. Whenever the dirty plates and cutlery piled up, he washed all of them before supper and started using the clean dishes and cutlery.

One day the wife met an American couple who were missionaries in her city. She connected with them in a deep way, and on that same day they shared with her the message of the gospel. She was powerfully struck by the love of God and was relieved from the fear of going to hell. As soon as she returned to her apartment, she was eager for her husband to come home so that she could tell him the good news. When her husband came home at five thirty, he went straight to the bedroom to drop off his briefcase, and he found that the bedroom was as untidy as always. He went to the kitchen to make tea and could not find one clean cup or glass. He realized that it was the night to wash all the piled-up dishes.

His wife joined him in the kitchen and, excited about the experience she had that day, started talking about her new American friends. She communicated to him how eager she was for him to meet them. She told him how she heard and understood what Jesus did on the cross and that she was worried about him — that he would go to hell if he did not believe in Christ. Her husband watched her quietly and thought to himself, *She is not only a self-centered and lazy woman, but now she has also become a religious freak.*

Suppose that on her insistence he goes with her to meet her American friends. Most likely his motives would be to psychoanalyze them to figure out what they do to influence foolish women to become religious freaks. In his attitude, he would be maligning the word of God.

Perhaps as you were reading this story, people you know came to your mind.

## THE SECOND SCENARIO

Let us imagine this same self-centered wife meeting the American couple and connecting with them very deeply. The connection was strong to the degree that they felt free to share with her the message of the gospel. As she had a deep realization of the truth about how much God loved her, all of a sudden she also had a deep understanding of how sinful she was. For the first time in her life, she realized that she was a very self-centered and lazy woman, and in tears she pleaded to God to forgive her. Upon returning to her apartment, she called her husband and told him that when he arrived home, she was going to tell him something very important.

The rest of that day she worked on cleaning the apartment for the first time. After hours of cleaning and washing the dishes and piled-up clothes, she decided she would like to cook something for her husband. Unfortunately, she did not have a clue about what he liked to eat, let alone how to cook it! So she called her mother-in-law, found out what his favorite meal was, and got the recipe. For the next couple of hours she worked in the kitchen.

When her husband returned home at five thirty, he smelled the aroma of his favorite meal coming from the kitchen. Rather than going to the bedroom to drop off his briefcase, he went straight to the kitchen and asked his wife, "Where is my mother?" She answered him, "Your mother is not here." So he asked her, "But who is cooking?" She responded by saying, "I am cooking." "But you do not know how to cook," he said. "Yes," she said, "but I called your mother and found out what you liked and got the recipe from her, and I hope it will taste the way you are used to."

That blew his mind. He went to the bedroom to drop off his brief-case and, to his amazement, found it was as tidy as it was on his first honeymoon night. *What happened to her?* he wondered. So he went back to the kitchen and asked her about the amazing change. In humility and brokenness she told him that she had met this American couple and they had told her about Jesus. Then she said to her husband, "I do not understand how you tolerated me all these months and did not divorce me. I wonder if you will ever be able to forgive me for my self-centeredness and laziness. Will you please forgive me?" "Of course I will," he said, "but tell me what happened and what motivated you to change." So she told him more about the American couple and how they talked to her about Jesus.

That evening was an unforgettable evening for him. Sitting at his dining room table, he actually ate his favorite meal cooked by his own wife. During the meal, he asked her questions about the American couple, and it seemed as if he was curious to meet them. He encouraged her to visit them whenever she wanted. He told her that she could go that same evening if she desired. In his case, he preferred to watch TV because he wanted to unwind and forget about his work. She told him she preferred to watch TV with him rather than going to the home of her new friends alone.

That evening the wife secretly made a huge decision. She decided to wake up at six rather than nine and fix breakfast for her husband. The next morning at six, for the first time in six months, she heard the alarm go off, but her inner clock was geared for her to wake up hours later. So she turned over and fell back to sleep. At seven she heard the door of the apartment close as her husband went to work, and she literally pulled herself out of bed. After she finished working in the apartment, she called her mother-in-law and asked her for more recipes of meals that her husband loved.

At five thirty her husband came back from work and had forgotten what happened the previous day. As soon as he opened the door of the apartment, he smelled the fragrance of another of his favorite meals and remembered what happened the day before.

Sooner or later, this husband would want to meet the American couple God used to change his wife. Upon visiting them, would he be maligning the Word of God as they shared with him the gospel? Of course not!

## Scenarios on Connecting with Muslims

Here, too, I will create two fictional situations that are really *composites* of situations of *real people* I have known in various parts of the world. They concern the wisdom of Paul in Titus 2:4-5. I myself will play a role in these two scenarios, and the composite character will be a young Egyptian man. This time the fictional treatments will focus on witnessing to Muslims. The first scenario describes a violation of the spirit of Titus 2:4-5, and the second scenario demonstrates what happens when the spirit of the commands of this passage are put into practice.

## The First Scenario

Let us imagine that during our years in Egypt, my wife and I had been asking God to connect us with Muslims who had a deep desire to know Christ and were willing to get into the Gospels to read His story. One day I met a university student in Cairo, Ali, who was an answer to our prayer. After spending some time with him, I found out that he had been looking for a New Testament and did not know how to get one. He did not dare go into churches and ask for an Injil. Furthermore, he knew of only one Christian bookstore in Cairo that might have it. But what if somebody who knows his family saw him going into that shop? What if he did not know how to ask for the Injil.? He was too embarrassed about his ignorance. So I told him that I had an extra copy and would love to give it to him. That day was the first time he had ever seen a New Testament. I showed him the table of contents, and I explained to him what we call chapters and verses and the difference between the Gospels and the Letters.

Then I asked him if he would be willing to get together once a week to go over the chapters he had read. He agreed to meet with me the following Tuesday. I asked him to share what he liked when he came, and I told him we would discuss together what he didn't understand. Furthermore, I told him not to tell anyone that he had met me or that he was reading the New Testament. He agreed to follow my advice and returned to his home.

His family was relatively well-off, and in their apartment he had his own bedroom. But he could not be sure his privacy would not be invaded. In Egypt it is quite acceptable for parents of the same sex to go into the bedrooms of their children without knocking on the door. So whenever Ali wanted to read in the New Testament, he would get under the blanket with his flashlight and New Testament and pretend that he was asleep.

Week after week he came to our apartment, and he was amazingly eager and yearning for a relationship with Christ. The times I shared with him were unforgettable. It is energizing and fun to see the Scriptures through the eyes of an honest and eager seeker.

Six months later Ali came to our home and told me that he had put his faith in Christ. We talked about it, and I found out that he had had a genuine encounter with Christ. I told my wife about it, and she congratulated him on the biggest decision of his life. Then I asked him whether he had told his parents about his decision, and he was surprised by my question. Because of my earlier advice, it seems he thought his relationship with Christ should remain a secret. So I shared with him the importance of telling his parents.

The next Tuesday he came to our home and poured out his excitement about the relevance of Christ to his life and about his motivation to study and become a better student. I asked him whether he had told his family about his faith in Christ. With shyness he told me that he did not have the courage to do so. I warned him that he needed to be careful not to be ashamed of Jesus. Then I shared with him how the young Christians in the book of Acts asked God for boldness and courage and that when they had the courage, they discovered many opportunities to witness about what Christ did in their lives. I encouraged him to tell his parents and even showed him what verse in the New Testament he could use when he talked with them.

Ali left our apartment that day sad and discouraged, yet he did not want to be ashamed of Jesus. When he reached home, he found his father in the sitting room quietly reading the Qur'an. Ali's knees were literally shaking with fear. He quietly went into his bedroom, got the New Testament from under his mattress, opened to the passage that I suggested, and put his thumb in that page. Then he went and sat quietly next to his dad so as not to interrupt his reading. After minutes of waiting, during which he could hear his heart pounding with fear, his father all of a sudden stopped reading and asked Ali, "Have you been going to the mosque to pray?" Ali said, "No." The father asked him, "Why not?" Ali's response was that he had become a Christian. The father could not believe his ears!

So Ali boldly started reading to his father the verse I had selected for him. With anger and screams, the father snatched the New Testament from Ali, tore it to pieces, and threw it from the window. Still screaming, the father expelled Ali from the house and told him that he was no longer his son. So Ali left the apartment and went down the stairs. His uncle next door heard the screaming and found out what happened. Ali heard his uncle say, "I will report him right away to the secret police."

A few hours later Ali came to our apartment. He told me the news about how he had been bold and courageous in witnessing and how his dad had expelled him from the house. Indirectly he was telling me that he had no place to stay and didn't know where to go. I congratulated him for his courage and assured him that Christ would take care of him. Then he told me that his uncle had gone to the secret police and reported him. When he told me this, I lost my peace. I began wondering whether the secret police had followed him and saw him coming to our home.

I had been planning to invite him to stay in our apartment until the situation at his home calmed down. But after he told me about his uncle, I thought it would be too dangerous to invite him to stay with us. So I excused myself and started calling friends of mine who had been praying for Ali for the past six months. I told them about Ali's predicament, especially with the secret police, but none of them agreed to let him stay at their homes. So I raised some money from those friends, and we decided to have him stay in a clean, cheap hotel until we could determine what to do with him. In the meantime, we started investigating the possibility of getting him a visa to America, Australia, or some other country. My friends and I came to the conclusion that it would be better for Ali and for us if he were to leave the country.

Although Ali is a fictional character, he is a composite of real people I know by name. His situation is a microcosm of the type of evangelism that has been taking place in the Muslim world for centuries. For one lady I know who endured a similar situation, it took sixteen years to restore her relationship with her extended family.

## THE SECOND SCENARIO

Let us imagine that one day I met the young man Ali after my wife and I had prayed for years that God would connect us with Muslims who were open and eager to know about Jesus. What an answer to prayer! After he shared with me his desire to have a New Testament, I offered him the extra copy I had. I showed him the table of contents in the New Testament and explained the difference between chapters and verses. Then I showed him my Bible and pointed out the table of contents in the Old Testament. I asked him if he would be willing to get together once a week in a certain place in downtown Cairo to go over what he had read. He was eager to do so.

I told him we would do that only if his parents would give him permission to meet with me. He looked at me with a strange expression on his face as if he were telling me, *Don't you know what my father will say? Do you come from a different planet?* So I opened my Bible to the book of Exodus and showed him the Ten Commandments. I explained that those Ten Commandments are a summary of the *Shari'a*, or the Law of God, in the Old Testament. We focused on the commandment to honor his father and mother, especially in light of the fact that he was still a student and his parents covered all his expenses.

I told him that we needed to be consistent, not obeying God in one area and bluntly disobeying Him in another. He turned to me and asked me whether I was really serious about his getting the permission of his parents. I said I was. That day I made two big mistakes: I forgot to get his phone number, and I forgot to ask him his family name. All I knew was that his name was Ali. I decided that when I saw him the following week, I would ask him for his family name and for his phone number.

The following Tuesday I went to the place where we were supposed to meet. He was not there. I waited for him for about an hour, and he still did not come. It was a very discouraging experience, but I came up with excuses such as, "Maybe he forgot our appointment." The following Tuesday I went again at the right time, and he still did not come. Again I was very discouraged for losing such a precious person, but I decided to pray for him every night before I went to sleep. I was prepared to pray for him for years. Faithfully, night after night, I asked God that He would connect Ali with others who could go with him on the rest of his journey to Christ.

Six months later I was in downtown Cairo and a miracle happened. In a city with millions of people I saw Ali by accident, or more correctly by providence. After praying for him on a daily basis for six months, I loved him and was overjoyed to see him. I gave him a big hug and asked him about our appointment six months earlier. He told me that he had obeyed the commandment of honoring his parents and told his dad about me. His father's response was, "Don't go to this man again." I told Ali that he did the right thing by obeying his dad, and I asked him how he was doing. He told me that one of his uncles had died the day before, and so many relatives had come from the south of Egypt for the funeral that their apartment was packed with people. I asked Ali whether it would be appropriate for me to go and give my condolences to his parents that evening. He thought that was a very good idea and gave me directions to his home.

For three evenings after the death of a relative, friends and relatives customarily go to the family to give their condolences. The women go up to the apartment while the men go to the makeshift tent in the shape of a very big room which is erected in the street in front of the building. The size of the makeshift tent varies according to how rich the family is. The bigger tents have the capacity to seat almost one hundred guests. When they build tents, they close the road, except for the sidewalk, and they create a detour for the traffic. The seats are arranged in a U shape. Facing them is a platform on which an Imam sits, reciting the Qur'an over a microphone. Above the tent they place huge loudspeakers so that the chanting of the Qur'an can be heard by the whole neighborhood. It is a way to announce to the neighborhood that it is the right time to come and give condolences. The custom is for the *Sheikh*, or Imam, to chant the Qur'an for about twenty minutes. Then they break for about half an hour. During the break, men converse with one another, but when the chanting resumes, people stop talking and listen respectfully.

That evening I drove to Ali's, and luckily, not far from his apartment I found a parking spot. As I walked toward it, the chanting of the Qur'an helped me quickly find the tent. When I entered the tent, I looked for Ali. He was sitting next to four other men, all wearing suits and neckties. The Sheikh was chanting the Qur'an, so I went toward Ali and his close male relatives, shook hands with them, and found a chair not far from the Sheikh.

Some Christians in Egypt, whether nominal or true believers, tend to be prejudiced against Muslims. I used to have that prejudice too, but God in His grace started healing me. When prejudiced Christians go to give their condolences to a Muslim family, they take a deep breath of "clean Christian air," hold their breath, and go in to visit. Their body language communicates very clearly that they are afraid of getting contaminated by the environment of Muslims while the Qur'an is being chanted.

In my case, I found a chair, sat down, and really enjoyed listening to the chanting of the Qur'an. The voice of the Sheikh was good, and the passage he was reciting was familiar to me. As I listened attentively, I asked myself whether what was being chanted was in agreement with what the Bible teaches or not. In the meantime, without my knowing it, Ali whispered to his dad and told him that I was the man who insisted that he ask for his dad's permission before seeing me and reading the Injil with me. Ali's father started observing me, and from my body language he saw that I was not "holding my nose" out of fear of getting contaminated.

When the Sheikh stopped chanting, I went to Ali and asked him to introduce me to his father. Right away, he and his dad created a space for me to sit between them. For the next twenty minutes I focused on Ali's dad and asked him questions: "How old was your brother? What was his sickness? Did he suffer a great deal? Did he have children, and how old are they? How is his wife doing?" The father was doing all the talking, and every now and then I asked a question. After that conversation, I felt that the purpose of the visit was accomplished, so I stood up to leave, shaking hands with the relatives of Ali as I walked out of the tent. To my surprise, not only Ali but also his dad came out of the tent to walk with me about ten or twenty meters to show their respect. They do that only with distinguished guests.

In response, I did what was expected. I stood with Ali and his dad and expressed my gratitude to them for wanting to honor me. I told them that they needed to go back to the tent in order to be with their guests, but they won the argument and walked with me for a while. Then I stopped them again and thanked them and insisted that they should return to their guests. This time I won, so I said good-bye to both of them again and went to look for my car. They walked back to the tent. Before I found my car, Ali came running with the great news that he asked his dad for permission to meet with me, and his father gave him permission.

Let us suppose that Ali and I got together on a weekly basis to read together the life of Christ, not for six months but for two and a half years before he put his faith in Christ. In the meantime, my wife and I got to know his family. We visited them several times, and they visited us as well. My wife got some recipes from his mother and gave private lessons in English to Ali's sister. Every Christmas and Easter, Ali's parents paid us a formal visit and even brought us gifts. They were very happy with the transformation that was taking place in the life of their son even before he declared his faith in Christ. His grades at the university were improving. His conduct at home changed dramatically. In the past, when his mother asked him to do some shopping for her on the way back from the university, he would yell at her, saying that he was very busy in his studies and that she should ask his sister to do the shopping.

Now a clear change of attitude had taken place. Before going to the university, Ali would ask his mother if she needed anything from the supermarket. The New Testament and the Bible that Ali possessed were not hidden under the mattress but were on his desk in his bedroom. At times he would leave them on the table in the sitting room. Sometimes his father or sister or mother would read them, and no one thought of it as wrong or unusual.

Finally, three years after our initial contact, Ali put his faith in

Christ. The six months after we first met were not a waste of time. I was praying for him on a daily basis. During the two and a half years we were reading the Bible together, I did not take him out of his context. At times his father would ask me questions about Christ based on what he was reading in the Bible. I was reaching not only Ali but his family as well. After Ali put his faith in Christ, he did not change his name to Steve or Peter. He was still Ali, who now loved Jesus and whose life was being transformed.

This story is fictional, but it is a composite of real people I know. It illustrates a type of evangelism that does not yank individuals out of their context but rather ministers to them within their context. In the next chapters, we will look at the Scriptures to see if this approach to ministry is allowed or even encouraged in the Bible. We will also look in greater detail at what it means to reach individuals in their context.

## QUESTIONS FOR REFLECTION AND DISCUSSION

1. Go back to the beginning of the chapter. What do you think of the Frenchman's statement? To what extent is Ahmad justified in what he said?

2. As you look at the seven commands in Titus 2:4-5, how can a wife who comes to know Christ influence the life of her nominal husband and draw him to Jesus? Do you know families who look more like the first scenario?

3. In the second set of scenarios regarding connecting with Muslims, do you know from experience people who fit one of the two composites? Does the second scenario have the ring of truth in it? In what way?

4. Can you think of a few texts in Scripture that teach that a person should not to be taken out of his or her context but should be given the opportunity to believe the gospel in a natural setting?

CHAPTER 15

# DIVERSITY OF MANIFESTATIONS

*For any Muslim to follow Christ he needs to forsake Islam, leave his family, join the church, and get integrated into Christianity. Anything less than that is a betrayal of Christ.*

— A SUDANESE CHRISTIAN

In response to the way Americans tried to convert him to Christianity, Ahmad said,

How can I give up my name, Ahmad, that was given to me when I was born and by which all my friends know me, and start being called Steve or Peter? How did you feel, as Americans, when you heard about the young American man, John Walker Lindh, who joined the Taliban in Afghanistan and took a Muslim name? By asking me to convert to Christianity, you are asking me to commit high treason.

At another time, Ahmad told one of his American friends, "When I visit your churches I do not feel that I belong. When I pray, I like to kneel and bow down before the almighty God along with others who are also willing to kneel and bow before God."

One of my favorite movies is the musical *Fiddler on the Roof*. It is the story of a Jewish family in Russia early in the twentieth century. Attempting to live a normal life filled with Jewish traditions, Tevye, a milkman, is searching for appropriate husbands for his three eldest daughters, Tzeitel, Hodel, and Chava. In a break of tradition, his daughters refuse to accept the wishes of the matchmaker and their father. Instead, they marry men they love. Tzeitel, the eldest daughter, marries a poor Jewish tailor. The father wishes that this first son-in-law had more money. Hodel, the second daughter, marries a Communist agnostic student from Kiev, who comes from a Jewish family. The father thinks they are both crazy but ultimately feels it's okay because this second son-in-law came from a Jewish family as well. Chava, the third daughter, marries the son of an Orthodox priest—a Christian. From Tevye's point of view, this third daughter committed high treason by marrying a Christian. He never talks to her again.

Muslims are very similar to Jews when it comes to changing religions. Ahmad told the Christians who were trying to convert him to Christianity, "By asking me to convert to Christianity, you are asking me to commit high treason." Does belief in Christ necessitate leaving Islam and getting integrated into Christianity? Can a Muslim believe wholeheartedly in Christ and yet remain among his own people as salt and light? That is what this chapter and the next will address.

In the Ali composite in the previous chapter, with the scenarios based on Titus 2:4-5, we saw the possibility of a Muslim having an encounter with Christ and developing a deep relationship with Him without having to commit "high treason." One of the major issues in helping a Muslim maintain the relationships God gave him or her over the years is having a fresh and new perspective of what church is and what it means to belong to the body of Christ. In this chapter, we will focus on the concept of *ekklesia* (church) and its various manifestations. In the next chapter, we will focus on the biblical basis of the phenomenon of the *hidden ekklesia*. In *Unshackled and Growing*, a book I wrote in 2006, I included a chapter on the subject of ekklesia. I am repeating this concept here because it is relevant to our discussion on faith and culture.[1]

## WHAT IS CHURCH?

If I were to show the following diagrams to Christians and ask them which one represents a church, most likely every one of them would point to diagram 1 because it describes the "obvious church."

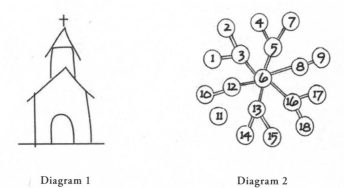

Diagram 1                    Diagram 2

When people, whether Christians or Muslims, think of church, what comes to their minds are various manifestations of the *obvious church* in the form of a building, distinct architecture, a gathering on Sunday morning, singing hymns, sitting in pews, collecting the offering, and so forth. All of that they may see in diagram 1.

But what about diagram 2? It represents the *hidden church*. Ekklesia means the people of God, and they can exist completely underground as a hidden church. The gospel in this ekklesia flows through channels of relationships quietly and effectively.

Diagram 2 is a set of personal networks. An individual such as 6 seems to be highly influential in this network, while 11 seems to be marginal. Both are precious to God. Furthermore, we see in diagram 2 that what connects the individuals with one another are double lines that represent channels of relationships. These channels could be either blocked or open.

Now consider diagram 2 as a relational network prior to anyone in the network coming to Christ. Suppose 6 became a follower of Christ. What would happen if 6 began to clear and strengthen these relational channels by becoming humble, asking for forgiveness when necessary, and reaching out to others in love as Jesus did? Can you imagine if this person refrained from self-righteous preaching at his family members and friends and instead let his lifestyle pave the way for him to articulate the gospel once he earned the right to speak? What if his life's mission among the people in his network was to live out the following two passages before he began to articulate the gospel?

Do not repay anyone evil for evil. Be careful to do what is right in the eyes of everybody. (Romans 12:17)

Give thanks in all circumstances, for this is God's will for you in Christ Jesus. (1 Thessalonians 5:18)

Can you envision the church as the people of God and not just a building or the meetings that take place there? What if 6, 3, and 16 in diagram 2 began a relationship with God, became unshackled from sin against others, and began growing? What would it take for all those in this diagram to become an ekklesia, which means "people of God"?* Can they remain in their own environment and still be an ekklesia? Are they an ekklesia if they don't move out into something that looks like diagram 1 (the obvious church) but instead share the good news of Christ through their relational channels? Does the Bible allow that? This question is very important, especially when we think of our Muslim brothers and sisters who have surrendered their lives to Christ in countries where leaving Islam is considered nothing less than high treason. Let's look at the New Testament ekklesia to see if we can find some answers.

## THE NEW TESTAMENT CHURCH

Has the ekklesia always looked like what we see today in the West? How did it start, and how did it evolve over the centuries?

We read about one of the earliest examples of the ekklesia after the Resurrection: "One day Peter and John were going up to the temple at the time of prayer—at three in the afternoon" (Acts 3:1). Peter and John, two disciples of Christ, continued to go to the Jewish temple, and it seems they went there at the set time of prayer. They were the ekklesia, the people of God, practicing their relationship with God and with one another in a Jewish context. Like Muslims who pray five times a day at set times, Jews also have established times for prayer. What does this verse say about how Peter and John perceived themselves? It seems they saw themselves as Jews who believed in Jesus. They did not perceive themselves as "Christians." (In fact, the term *Christian* was not

---

* The Greek word for church is *ekklesia*, meaning "the called out people of God." The ekklesia is very special to God, and in the Bible it is spoken of as the family of God, the body of Christ, and the temple of the Holy Spirit. Another important Greek word that is repeated in the New Testament is *oikos*, which is usually translated as "household." The oikos, or household, was the social structure in existence during New Testament times. In the first few centuries, the ekklesia penetrated the social structure of the time, namely the oikos.

in existence at the time.) Believing in Jesus did not make it necessary for them to leave the temple. After the resurrection of Christ and His ascension to heaven, His followers, the ekklesia, began to be persecuted in Jerusalem. For example, one disciple, Stephen, was stoned to death. Acts 8 describes it this way: "On that day a great persecution broke out against the church at Jerusalem, and all except the apostles were scattered throughout Judea and Samaria. . . . Those who had been scattered preached the word wherever they went" (verses 1,4).

Up to that point, the scattered followers of Christ preached the word only to Jews, their own people. But in Antioch a transition took place:

> Now those who had been scattered by the persecution in connection with Stephen traveled as far as Phoenicia [Lebanon], Cyprus and Antioch [Antioch is a city by the eastern shore of the Mediterranean Sea, north of Syria], telling the message only to Jews. Some of them, however, men from Cyprus and Cyrene [Libya], went to Antioch and began to speak to Greeks also, telling them the good news about the Lord Jesus. (Acts 11:19-20)

At this stage, the ekklesia, the people of God who met together in Antioch, included not only believers in Christ from a Jewish background but also some from a Gentile or non-Jewish background.

Later, when the apostle Paul carried the gospel to Turkey and Greece, everywhere he went he started at the town synagogue. The only exception was in the city of Philippi because there was no synagogue in that city. There, Jewish worshipers and their friends went to a place near a river to learn about God. So that's where Paul went in Philippi, sticking with his practice of starting with Jews. He wanted to tell them that the Messiah they had been waiting for had come, and He was the Lord Jesus Christ.

Some Jews in these cities came to faith in Christ, while others started opposing Paul and persecuting Christ's followers. In time, more and more Gentiles began believing in Christ, so much so that Paul's primary ministry shifted to the Gentiles. To the church in Ephesus, where the majority were Gentile-background believers and where Paul spent the longest time of his ministry, he wrote about unity in the ekklesia in spite of diversity:

Therefore, remember that formerly you who are Gentiles by birth and called "uncircumcised" by those who call themselves "the circumcision" (that done in the body by the hands of men) — remember that at that time you [Gentile followers of Christ] were separate from Christ, excluded from citizenship in Israel and foreigners to the covenants of the promise, without hope and without God in the world. But now in Christ Jesus you who once were far away have been brought near through the blood of Christ.

For he himself [Jesus Christ] is our [believers in Christ from Jewish and Gentile backgrounds] peace, who has made the two one and has destroyed the barrier, the dividing wall of hostility, by abolishing in his flesh the law with its commandments and regulations. His purpose was to create in himself one new man out of the two, thus making peace, and in this one body to reconcile both of them to God through the cross, by which he put to death their hostility. He came and preached peace to you who were far away [Gentile believers] and peace to those who were near [Jewish believers]. For through him we both [Jewish and Gentile believers] have access to the Father by one Spirit.

Consequently, you are no longer foreigners and aliens, but fellow citizens with God's people and members of God's household, built on the foundation of the apostles and prophets, with Christ Jesus himself as the chief cornerstone. (Ephesians 2:11-20)

Please look carefully at diagram 3 in light of Ephesians 2:11-20.

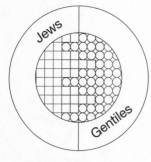

**Diagram 3**

What do you observe in this diagram? The outer circle contains both Jews and Gentiles; the Jews are depicted as *squares*, while the Gentiles are depicted as *circles*, with a wall of hostility separating them.* But does that wall exist in the inner circle, the family of God, the ekklesia? It does not. The squares, representing Jews, and the circles, representing Gentiles, live side by side, brothers and sisters within the family of God. But notice how the circles do not need to become squares to belong to the kingdom of God, and the squares do not need to become circles, either. There is *unity in the midst of diversity*. Note that the two peoples, though one in the body of Christ, appear to be segregated. This may strike you as strange, but it will become clear as you read this chapter and the next, noticing why this is sometimes necessary in taking the gospel to people of another faith.

## IMPLICATIONS FOR TODAY

What does the family of God look like today? *Must there be uniformity to achieve unity?* Should all the circles become squares in order to have unity in the ekklesia?

---

\* In my teaching at seminaries, I use diagrams with colors. I often talk about blue squares and green circles. Since I cannot use colors in this book, I will talk about squares and circles without the colors. No pun is intended with the word *square*. Actually, in the context of this chapter, I come from a square background that goes back to Constantine.

We looked at the Gentile/Jew controversy during Paul's time. Can we find similarities to our situation today? Certainly we can if we replace Jews and Gentiles in the diagram with Christians and Muslims. Notice diagram 4:

Christians in this diagram have twenty centuries of history. Many of them today are nominal Christians who do not have an intimate relationship with Christ. But those who do surrender their lives to Christ enter the ekklesia, the inner circle, and maintain their Christian *square background*. There are also Muslims who have surrendered their lives to Christ and have entered the ekklesia, the inner circle, with their Muslim *circle background*. In the ekklesia, there is no wall of hostility separating the *squares* from the *circles*, even though we are very aware of the wall of hostility that exists between Christians and Muslims who are outside the ekklesia, or the family of God.

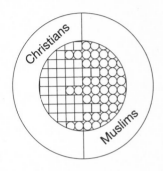

Diagram 4

Now go back to Ephesians 2:11-20 and read this passage again, replacing the word *Jew* with the word *Christian* and the word *Gentile* with the word *Muslim*. The first time I did this, years ago, the New Testament took on new relevance.

> Therefore, remember that formerly you [followers of Christ from a Muslim background — circles] who are [Muslims] by birth . . . — remember that at that time you were separate from Christ. . . . But now in Christ Jesus you who once were far away have been brought near through the blood of Christ.
>
> For he himself [Jesus Christ] is our [believers in Christ from Christian and Muslim backgrounds] peace, who has made the two one and has destroyed the barrier, the

dividing wall of hostility, by abolishing in his flesh the law with its commandments and regulations. His purpose was to create in himself one new man out of the two, thus making peace, and in this one body to reconcile both of them to God through the cross, by which he put to death their hostility. He came and preached peace to you who were far away [followers of Christ from a Muslim circle background] and peace to those who were near [followers of Christ from a Christian square background]. For through him we both [followers of Christ from Christian and Muslim backgrounds] have access to the Father by one Spirit.

Consequently, you [followers of Christ from a Muslim background] are no longer foreigners and aliens, but fellow citizens with God's people and members of God's household, built on the foundation of the apostles and prophets, with Christ Jesus himself as the chief cornerstone.

What do you think? What insights are you getting? God loves diversity. (Just look around!) He does not intend for us all to be alike. Rather, He desires to destroy the wall of hostility and reconcile all of us to Himself and to one another through the cross. There *can be* unity in spite of diversity in the ekklesia. It was true in the first century, and it's true today.

## EKKLESIA MANIFESTATIONS TODAY

I have learned that in one of the Muslim countries I have visited repeatedly, Muslims who put their faith in Jesus Christ (*Isa Al Masih*) can exist at three different levels with three different manifestations of the ekklesia.

The first manifestation is the *obvious church*. This is a church above the ground and is recognized by a building, obvious leadership, traditions, and certain times during the week when Christians come together to meet, as we see in diagram 1.

In this diagram, I present the Christians who belong to the *obvious church* as squares. They have their distinct Christian culture and language. Muslim-background believers who join this *obvious church* tend to make a complete exodus from Islam and its distinct culture and put on the *obvious-church* culture. The overwhelming majority of these churches are made up of national Christians, squares, with a sprinkling of Muslim-background believers in Christ.* These MBBs used to be circles with Muslim names but have become squares with new Christian names. For example, Ishaku (a circle) becomes Isaac (a square), and Ahmad becomes Steve. The governments in these Muslim countries know about these MBBs and might keep a tight control over them by watching them closely.

Diagram 1

A second ekklesia manifestation is the *semihidden church*, depicted in diagram 5.

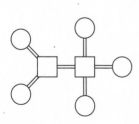

Diagram 5

Here we see two squares who might be either missionaries or national Christians. One of the two missionaries is in contact with three Muslims (circles) who have become followers of Christ. The other is in touch with two Muslims (circles) who have put their faith in Christ. These five MBBs, who are still circles, have never met one another. But the two squares,

---

* These national Christians could be Egyptian Christians in Egypt and Chinese Christians in Indonesia.

the missionaries or the national Christians, are under real or imagined pressure to *plant a church*. So they bring together, for the first time, their five Muslim contacts (circles) who have believed in Christ.

We see in diagram 5 that in the first meeting of these seven people, there is no relationship among the circles. The only reason those five MBBs (the circles) came to the meeting is because their Christian friends, the squares, invited them. In this first meeting, the fellowship centers around the missionaries or the national Christians. The MBBs tend to be silent and reserved because they are suspicious of one another. What if one of the five circles is an undercover member of the secret police? Under such circumstances, it is best and safest for these circles to remain quiet. Those who do the talking will be the two squares. This semihidden church has the potential of becoming an *obvious church* (see diagram 1) or a *hidden church* (see diagram 2). It all depends on what those missionaries or national Christians do with their Muslim contacts. Will they invite them to their square comfort zones, or will the missionaries develop within themselves circular Muslim hearts and encourage the MBBs to continue to be connected with their families and friends, as we saw in diagram 2 the *hidden church*.

This *hidden church* is completely underground and is made up entirely of circles already connected to one another by existing relationships based on family or friendship ties. If there are any missionaries

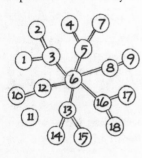

Diagram 2

or national Christians who are connected with people in the *hidden church*, they are connected only with a few leaders. Those Christians are squares with very circular hearts. Like Barnabas, who listened to Paul and became his advocate in the Jerusalem church, these Christians believe in the circles and become their advocates among the leadership of the *square obvious churches*. Like Barnabas, who recruited

Paul and on the first journey together allowed him to lead, these Christians encourage the MBBs to develop and lead. These squares with circular hearts have *no ulterior motives* to *transform the circles into squares* or to make the *hidden church* surface and become an *obvious church*. The hidden church spreads quietly through relationships, like yeast in the dough (see Matthew 13:33), and it is rapidly growing.*

## A GENTILE OIKOS

All of Acts 10 and more than half of Acts 11 speak in detail about a Gentile who is the head of an oikos (household). His name is Cornelius. These two chapters describe how among the Gentiles there are honest seekers in whom God is at work. These chapters also show how God's people are hesitant to cross boundaries to unfamiliar realms to see how God is at work in His ekklesia in a different setting, namely in the social structures that existed in the first century.

Cornelius was a Roman who belonged to a distinguished family. He was a man of importance in Caesarea and was well known to the Jews (see 10:22). A centurion in the Italian cohort, Cornelius was the captain of one hundred soldiers, mostly Italians.

Cornelius stands out as a devout and God-fearing Gentile against a backdrop of decadent polytheism. He yearned for a relationship with God and embraced the monotheism of the Jews. He read their Scriptures and practiced some Jewish rites. His faith was demonstrated by prayer at regular hours and by alms to the Jews. He was the head of an oikos that must have included not only his extended family but soldiers, servants, and possibly friends as well (see 10:27). I have heard it estimated that Cornelius's oikos numbered between twenty-five

---

* Some people refer to the circles as "insiders" and to the squares with circular hearts as "alongsiders."

and one hundred. Diagram 2 that we looked at earlier in this chapter describes Cornelius's oikos. His oikos was typical of the social structures that existed at that time.

The significance of the story of Cornelius and his household is that Cornelius was not a proselyte (a convert to Judaism), nor was he circumcised under the law (see 10:28,34,45; 11:3,18). He was a devout Gentile who adopted some Jewish ideas and customs. The book of Acts calls him "God-fearing" (10:2). Most likely he was the first Gentile who entered the *front door* of the ekklesia without first going through the *narrow gate of the Jewish religion*. This incident settled the fundamental question of unity in spite of diversity within the ekklesia of Christ.

Like Cornelius, there are Muslims in the deep corners of the Muslim world who are yearning for a relationship with Christ. We hear only of a few of them. One particular person I know was attracted to Christ as he read the Qur'an. The abundance of verses that talk about Christ and Mary in the Qur'an motivated him to look for and get a New Testament. This person belonged to a social structure, an extended family, similar to the *oikoi** that existed in the first century. When these Muslims come to know Christ, they can become salt and light among their own people as they *focus on cleaning the channels of relationships* and *living Christlike lifestyles before they rush into articulating the gospel through words*.

The ekklesia in Jerusalem struggled with the phenomenon of Cornelius. Peter hesitated before obeying God. God had to miraculously convince Peter to accept the command to go to the home of the Gentile and possibly eat Gentile food (see Acts 10:10-20). Knowing how risky it was to obey God by going outside the boundaries of the familiar Jewish culture, Peter took with him six witnesses (see 11:12). When Peter was later interrogated by the church leaders in Jerusalem

---

* *Oikoi* is plural for oikos.

(see 11:2-3), he had to justify his obedience to God (see 11:4-14). He put all the blame on God: "As I began to speak, the Holy Spirit came on them as he had come on us at the beginning. . . . So if God gave them the same gift as he gave us, who believed in the Lord Jesus Christ, who was I to think that I could oppose God?" (11:15,17).

We face similar challenges today that the church of Christ faced in the first century. There are Christian brothers and sisters around the world who echo what our Sudanese brother said at the beginning of this chapter: "For any Muslim to follow Christ he needs to forsake Islam, leave his family, join the church, and get integrated into Christianity. Anything less than that is a betrayal of Christ." Is it really a betrayal of Christ? Or is it more accurately a betrayal of our Christian customs and traditions?

In this chapter we looked at some biblical texts that show that unity can exist in the ekklesia in spite of diversity. In the next chapter we will look at other texts.

## REFLECTION AND DISCUSSION QUESTIONS

1. Go back to the beginning of the chapter. What do you think of the statements made by Ahmad and the Sudanese Christian about high treason and betrayal?
2. Matthew 18:20 says, "For where two or three come together in my [Jesus'] name, there am I with them." In light of this verse, what are the minimum essentials for an ekklesia in an *oikos* setting?
3. How did the apostle Paul cross the boundaries to the unfamiliar and enter the Gentile culture? What can we learn from 1 Corinthians 9:19-21 in our contexts?
   "Though I am free and belong to no man, I make myself a slave to everyone, to win as many as possible. To the Jews I became like a Jew, to win the Jews. To those under the law I became like one

under the law (though I myself am not under the law), so as to win those under the law. To those not having the law I became like one not having the law (though I am not free from God's law but am under Christ's law), so as to win those not having the law."

4. Consider an oikos as portrayed by diagram 2. What passages in the Bible talk about remaining as salt and light in one's context (staying circles rather than becoming squares)? What are some principles we can glean from them?

# CHAPTER 16

# REMAINING
# IN CONTEXT

*Can you imagine a Satan worshiper staying in his Satan worshipers' church in order to be salt and light among his own people? Islam is evil, and no one can stay within Islam as an insider.*

— A SYRIAN CHRISTIAN

My friend Ahmad wrote, *"If I were to leave Islam and become integrated into Christianity, I would lose my authenticity among my own people. Not only would my people see me as a traitor, but I would have the same perception myself! . . . Can you imagine the shame that my family and friends would feel if I were to leave Islam and get integrated into Christianity?"*

Let me present a fictional situation in which I play the role of a composite. Imagine me as an Egyptian Christian, a true believer living in Cairo.*

Every Thursday evening, I go to our Protestant church in downtown Cairo to attend the meeting for working men and women. Because I was discriminated against during my university days, I have a certain prejudice against Muslims. In our Egyptian newspapers, we often read articles written by Muslims attacking Christianity and the Bible. Furthermore, a Muslim equivalent of a TV evangelist keeps insulting our religion.

On a certain Thursday, I go to our weekly meeting at church. My friends tell me that we have a guest speaker tonight, a Muslim who has become a Christian. My response to the news is a mixture of pleasure and suspicion. Is he a genuine Christian, or is he playing a role in order to deceive us? When he enters the church, he automatically repulses me as I notice that he has a bruise on his forehead, a hypocritical manifestation of his fake spirituality. Fanatical Muslims with a *zibeeba* (a bruise on the forehead) attempt to communicate the message that they have prayed so many times, kneeling and touching the carpet with their foreheads, that they got that bruise. Another thing that repulses me is the way he greets me. He says, *"Asalamu 'alaykum"* (peace to you). Only Muslims use that terminology when they greet one another. Perhaps he is not a true Christian. Something that repulses me even more is his name. How could he come to our church with the Muslim name Mustafa? Mustafa means "the chosen one" and is one of the names of their prophet Muhammad because they believe that he was chosen by God. I wonder what kind of meeting we will be having tonight.

After the singing and the prayers, this man is introduced as a former Muslim who has become a Christian. I sit there wondering whether my

---

*   In reality, I come from a Lebanese background, but I lived with my family in Egypt for fifteen years.

friends who invited him were duped and trusted him prematurely. I need him to convince me that he has become a "real and true Christian," just like me, and I am not an easy person to convince.

When he starts sharing his story, I, like most of those in the church meeting, quietly listen to him to find out whether he is genuine. As he warms up and starts attacking Islam and ridiculing Muhammad and the Muslim faith, I start enjoying his story. From our laughter at his jokes about Islam and our agreeing with him about his attacks, he finds out how to win our approval. By the time he finishes, we are all elated and encouraged by his sharing, although we wish he were more polished like us and used our Christian terminology. But we know we need to be patient because this polish will come with time and practice. After the meeting, I, along with others, thank him for his sharing and congratulate him on his conversion. As people come and thank him, he feels as though he has finally found his place of belongingness in our church meeting because he is being treated like a hero with a halo around his head.

I still do not like the zibeeba, the bruise on his forehead. I hope that in the future he will put cream on it in order to cover it up. During the informal time at the end of the meeting, I follow him with the corner of my eye and notice at one point that he is talking to my younger sister and to other women. When I see him doing that, I begin to wonder about his motives. Is he coming after the women? Why would a Muslim want to believe in Christ other than for women, money, or a desire to go to America? So back at home, I warn my sister and advise her not to get too excited just yet that he has become a true believer. We will need to wait and see "fruit" before we trust him. I even quote to her the litmus test: "By their fruit you will recognize them" (Matthew 7:20).

When Mustafa returns the following Thursday to our church meeting, not as the speaker but as an ordinary person, he finds that most of us respond to him with plastic, artificial smiles. We keep him away at a safe distance because he still greets us by saying *"Asalamu 'alaykum,"* and he still "smells" like a Muslim. It seems I was not the only one from our group who preached to a family member a little sermon about the need to avoid Mustafa until we see fruit! So Mustafa starts wondering whether he has come to the right church. Very soon he meets another Protestant Christian in Cairo, who invites him to his church. The halo returns temporarily but does not last long. Then he gets invited to another church and to another, and in the meantime he learns how to please the Christians: by making fun of Islam and by attacking Muhammad and the Qur'an.

As the months pass, he begins to get more polished in his terminology. At the same time, he ruptures every relationship he had with his Muslim family and friends as he becomes openly critical of Islam. He even changes his name from Mustafa to Peter and gets baptized. Shortly afterward, he comes to our Thursday meeting again, this time to give a testimony of how he is suffering for Christ. He is not Mustafa anymore, but brother Peter. I never felt at ease by calling him "brother Mustafa." *Brother* and *Mustafa* did not mesh. He no longer uses the Muslim terminology he used to, and he lifts up his arms in church during the singing and shouts, "Hallelujah" and "Praise the Lord." Now he has really become one of us; he is inside our "fortress with thick walls" that protects us from the Muslims outside.

This composite sadly describes how we Christians, who tend to be very square in our culture, have treated Muslim-background believers over the centuries. Does the Bible teach that a Muslim, upon believing in Christ, should rupture his relationships with his Muslim family and friends and get integrated into Christianity? Is it possible for a Muslim-background believer in Christ to remain among his own people?

## NAAMAN'S DILEMMA

In chapter 14 we looked at a fictional character, Ali, who was a composite of real people, in light of Titus 2:4-5. Also, in chapter 15 we looked at how Paul addressed the issue of unity in spite of diversity within the ekklesia (see Ephesians 2:11-20). Now we want to look at a related issue in the Old Testament in which faith in God did not necessitate losing position or influence but rather encouraged remaining in context with relationships intact.

We read in Acts 10 about the Gentile Cornelius; now we want to look at the Gentile Naaman in 2 Kings 5. Naaman was the commander of the army of Syria during the time of Elisha the prophet. He was a rich man with great influence, and he was a war hero, beloved by the king of Syria, who made his power available to him. Yet despite his tremendous power and prestige, Naaman had a huge problem. He was sick with leprosy. However, he did not lose his job, nor was he banished from the company of people.

Furthermore, Naaman was a man of faith. He was also a humble man who admitted his need, and he was obedient. He believed what his Israelite slave told him about Elisha, the prophet in Israel, and he translated his faith into action by talking to the king and asking for permission to go and visit the prophet in order to seek healing from his disease.

So the king of Syria wrote a letter to the king of Israel: "With this letter I am sending my servant Naaman to you so that you may cure him of his leprosy" (verse 6). While he was in Israel, Naaman, in obedience to the prophet Elisha "went down and dipped himself in the Jordan seven times, as the man of God had told him, and his flesh was restored and became clean like that of a young boy" (verse 14).

Naaman experienced the miracle of healing from leprosy and at the same time came to a deep faith in *Yahweh*, the God of Israel. But he had a dilemma: How could he worship *Yahweh* the God of Israel while he was living in Damascus? How could he avoid worshiping idols and yet maintain his position of influence with Aram, the king of Syria? This was his burning issue.

It seems that King Aram liked Naaman, so whenever he went to the temple to worship the god Rimmon, the king wanted Naaman to go with him. On approaching the statue of Rimmon in the temple, the king, while leaning on Naaman's arm, had to kneel in front of the statue. Naaman had to kneel too, for he could not detach himself from the king without offending the king's honor. This was the cause of Naaman's concern. After his healing, Naaman had come to the conclusion that only Yahweh was God, and Rimmon was merely an idol. He also came to the conclusion that he should not worship Rimmon. At the same time, he did not want to lose his position of influence in Syria by moving to Israel so that he could worship Yahweh.

So Naaman went to Elisha the prophet and presented to him his burning issue. After explaining his dilemma, he said,

> Please let me, your servant, be given as much earth as a pair of mules can carry, for your servant will never again make burnt offerings and sacrifices to any other god but the LORD. But may the LORD forgive your servant for this one thing: When my master enters the temple of Rimmon to bow down and he is leaning on my arm and I bow there also — when I bow down in the temple of Rimmon, may the LORD forgive your servant for this. (verses 17-18)

Elisha's response was, "Go in peace" (verse 19). In essence, Elisha told Naaman to go back to Damascus and to go with the king to the temple of Rimmon and not to worry about kneeling with the king. In doing so, he could maintain his position of influence.

The passages in 2 Kings 5 and Acts 10–11 are illustrative passages that describe people — they are not teaching passages. We cannot build teaching principles upon them. At the same time, they illustrate to us how people through the centuries limited God to certain geography or to familiar boundaries. Naaman assumed that Yahweh was limited to

Israel and thought perhaps that if he could take some dirt from Israel with him back to Damascus, he would bring Yahweh along as well, or at least Yahweh would be willing to manifest His presence there.

This was the problem of the Samaritan woman in John 4 as well, and it is the problem of many Christians who limit God's presence to our Christian places of worship and to our Christian activities. Jesus said to the Samaritan woman,

> Believe me, woman, a time is coming when you will worship the Father neither on this mountain nor in Jerusalem. . . . A time is coming and has now come when the true worshipers will worship the Father in spirit and truth, for they are the kind of worshipers the Father seeks. God is spirit, and his worshipers must worship in spirit and in truth. (John 4:21,23-24)

Many of us Christians limit God to our "Christian geography" and expect Muslims to *join our Christianity* in order to be genuine Christians. We expect them to become photocopies of us before we can trust them. We expect them to endorse our twenty centuries of history rather than the *truths* and *practices* we find in the Bible. We thus limit God's action to that which takes place within the walls of our churches. We often limit the ekklesia to diagram 1 that we looked at in the beginning of the previous chapter.

Naaman's story is an *illustrative text*. Now we want to look carefully at a *teaching text* from the Scriptures on the issue of remaining in context with relationships intact.

## A NUGGET OF TRUTH

One time I used 1 Corinthians 7:17-24 to teach about the need for Muslim believers in Christ to remain as salt and light among their own people. After the message, someone came to me and told me that

I had no right to use that text to speak about Muslims remaining in their contexts. That text, he told me, was in the middle of a chapter that talks about marriage and about marriage only. So I went back and studied that chapter more in depth. I came to a deeper conviction that 1 Corinthians 7:17-24 not only speaks to the issue of marriage but addresses other issues as well, including the issue of remaining in context. It has become one of the main texts in the Scriptures that I use for addressing this approach to ministry.

Paul starts 1 Corinthians 7 by addressing the value of remaining single. At times Paul sounds very gentle and not forceful at all in his opinions: "I say this as a concession, not as a command" (verse 6). As Paul continues to address issues related to marriage, he comes to a sticky issue: What if a woman comes to faith in Christ, and her husband is not a believer? Should she divorce him? He answers this issue by saying, "If a woman has a husband who is not a believer and he is willing to live with her, she must not divorce him" (verse 13). Then Paul goes on to give his reasoning: "For the unbelieving husband has been sanctified through his wife, and the unbelieving wife has been sanctified through her believing husband. Otherwise your children would be unclean, but as it is, they are holy" (verse 14). (I found his reasoning difficult to understand until I connected this passage with 1 Peter 3:1-6, which I will come to soon.) Then Paul goes on to say, "But if the unbeliever leaves, let him do so. A believing man or woman is not bound in such circumstances; God has called us to live in peace. How do you know, wife, whether you will save your husband? Or, how do you know, husband, whether you will save your wife?" (verses 15-16).

It seems that the ultimate purpose in Paul's mind was for the believing partner to remain in the marriage in the hope that the other partner would come to know Christ. To give his argument more power, Paul resorted to one of his theological "nuggets" that fits not only this chapter but other chapters in other letters as well. The theological nugget he resorted to is found in 1 Corinthians 7:17-24* and is captured succinctly in verse 20: "Each one should remain in the situation which he was in when God called him."

Once Paul dealt with the issue of the believing partner and then clarified his reasoning by resorting to the nugget in 1 Corinthians 7:17-24, he then dealt in the rest of the chapter with family life issues and the need to live life in light of the brevity of time and the importance of our mission.

I will start my discussion of this issue by going to the very helpful cross-reference in 1 Peter 3:1-6 and will then come back and focus on the nugget in 1 Corinthians 7:17-24.

## THE CROSS-REFERENCE

The reason 1 Peter 3:1-6 is a helpful cross-reference is because it talks about a wife who is a true believer, while her husband is either a nonbeliever or a mediocre Christian. Here is what Peter wrote on this subject:

> Wives, in the same way be submissive to your husbands so that, if any of them do not believe the word, they may be won over without words by the behavior of their wives, when they see the purity and reverence of your lives. Your beauty should not come from outward adornment, such as braided hair and the wearing of gold jewelry and fine clothes. Instead, it should be that of your inner self, the unfading beauty of a gentle and quiet spirit, which is of great worth in God's sight. For this

---

\* There are other nuggets Paul used the same way in the rest of his letters that could fit into almost any of his letters. The two most famous are Philippians 2:5-11 and Colossians 1:15-20. Most probably these nuggets were memorized by the early church and sung as hymns.

is the way the holy women of the past who put their hope in God used to make themselves beautiful. They were submissive to their own husbands, like Sarah, who obeyed Abraham and called him her master. You are her daughters if you do what is right and do not give way to fear.

Peter started out by defining the situation the believing wife was in with her mediocre husband and suggested that she should submit to him in order to win him to Christ through the beauty of her life. Submission is not subservience. Submission implies being aware of God and His dealings in our lives. Being preoccupied with the person we are submitting to, rather than being aware of God, results either in subservience or inner rebellion.

In verses 3-4, Peter speaks about submission as inner beauty, a beauty that does not fade with age. Submission is like a precious painting; the adornments that women choose are like the frame. The frame should enhance the beauty of the painting rather than compete with it.

Peter then comes to verses 5-6 and encourages Christian women to consider Sarah as the model par excellence in the Old Testament on how to be submissive to one's husband. Why not Ruth? Ruth submitted not only to her husband but also to her mother-in-law even after the death of her husband! Was Sarah a model of submission? It seems that Abraham submitted to her more than she submitted to him during the conflict with Hagar.

In two incidents that we know of, however, Sarah submitted to her husband, even when he was wrong. In Genesis 20, Abraham asked his wife to go to Abimelech to save his own neck. Sarah could have said to God, "Lord, I accept the fact that Abraham is my husband and as the head of the family he is supposed to carry an umbrella of leadership and protect the whole family. But now he is not worthy of carrying that umbrella. Actually, his umbrella is all torn and the rain is pouring on me. Why should I stay under that umbrella? I want to walk out."

But instead, Sarah submitted to Abraham and went to the palace of Abimelech. And God came with His big beach umbrella and placed it above the umbrella of the "mediocre" Abraham. He protected Sarah by preventing Abimelech from having sex with her because she chose to submit to her husband and trust God.* What both Peter and Paul were saying to the believing partner is to stay married to the unbelieving partner and seek to win him or her to Christ. Then Paul went into a crescendo by appealing to his big gun, the nugget found in 1 Corinthians 7:17-24.

## THE BIG GUN

Let us look carefully at this nugget:

> [17]Nevertheless, each one should retain the place in life that the Lord assigned to him and to which God has called him. This is the rule I lay down in all the churches. Was a man already circumcised when he was called? He should not become uncircumcised. [18]Was a man uncircumcised when he was called? He should not be circumcised. [19]Circumcision is nothing and uncircumcision is nothing. Keeping God's commands is what counts. [20]Each one should remain in the situation which he was in when God called him. [21]Were you a slave when you were called? Don't let it trouble you—although if you can gain your freedom, do so. [22]For he who was a slave when he was called by the Lord is the Lord's freedman;

---

* At times submission takes a different direction manifested in courage, for example when an abused person does not accept the abuse and practices tough love.

similarly, he who was a free man when he was called is Christ's slave. [23]You were bought at a price; do not become slaves of men. [24]Brothers, each man, as responsible to God, should remain in the situation God called him to.

In verse 17 Paul starts very forcefully. He is no longer making gentle suggestions as he did in verse 6: "I say this as a concession, not as a command." In verse 17 he is saying that remaining in context is an *assignment* from God and a *calling* by Him. If one refuses to remain in the situation he was in when God called him, he is risking abandoning God's assignment and calling. Then he says that retaining that place in life is a principle that he teaches and lays down in all the churches. Actually, he repeats this principle in this short text three times: in verses 17, 20, and 24.

Paul then goes into two areas of life in which this principle applies in addition to marriage. It applies also to the Jew/Gentile controversy and to the issue of slavery. To the Jew who has become a believer in Christ, he tells him not to become a Gentile Christian. To the Gentile Christian, he tells him not to go and get circumcised and become a Jewish Christian. Being Jewish or being Gentile is nothing. What counts is surrender to Christ and retaining one's own identity and enjoying one's own skin. In the following diagrams we see that what really matters is not whether the Christian is a square or a circle. What really matters is for that person to belong to the inner circle of the ekklesia.

As we saw earlier, we can look at this diagram of the Jews and Gentiles and replace the word *Jews* with *Christians* and *Gentiles* with *Muslims*. The Muslim does not have to change his shape and identity in order to enter the kingdom of God. He can enter directly into the *wide gate of the kingdom*, rather than through our *narrow gate of twenty*

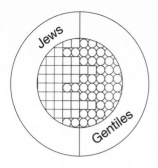
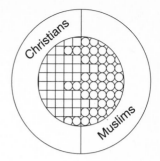

*centuries of Christian identity and traditions.* As we saw with the stories of Cornelius and Naaman, they did not need to change their shape and become squares in order to enter the kingdom of God.

Then Paul comes to another issue that must have been a burning issue in his day, namely slavery. What if a slave comes to know Christ, and his owner is a believer in Christ as well? Should the Christian slave demand his liberation? How does Paul address that issue? He tells the Christian slave, starting with verse 21, "Were you a slave when you were called? Don't let it trouble you—although if you can gain your freedom, do so. For he who was a slave when he was called by the Lord is the Lord's freedman; similarly, he who was a free man when he was called is Christ's slave. You were bought at a price; do not become slaves of men."

Paul is saying to the Christian slave that it would be great if he can gain his freedom. But if he cannot, he should not indulge in self-pity with a victim mentality, resenting his boss, who is his owner. Paul reminds the slave that he is a free man on the inside and motivates him to focus on the freedom he already possesses. Then he reminds him that his boss who owns him is, after all, a slave of Christ. In other words, we live in an unjust and broken world, but as we stand before Christ, the ground is level. So he tells this slave, repeating the same principle for the third time, to retain the place in life that the Lord assigned to him and to which God has called him and thus embrace his circumstances rather than resent them.

First Corinthians 7:21-24 has to do with slavery, but in many parts of the world slavery has been abolished. Does this text still have relevance to our world today?

In Egypt there are three distinct classes of society: a very small class of very rich people; a somewhat larger class, which we call the middle class; and a very large segment of society that people refer to as the lower class.

A young man with the name Ramzi grew up in the lower class in a very poor area of Cairo. His family was Protestant, and he faithfully attended the meetings at a small Protestant church in that poor part of the city. Ramzi was very involved in church activities and at a young age put his faith in Christ. He was a very serious student and got the best grades. In his high school government exam, he got excellent results, which qualified him to enter medical school. At government universities in Egypt, the education is free. At medical school Ramzi came to know a classmate, a young lady with the name Layla, who had a very similar background, having grown up in a poor Protestant family in another poor area of Cairo. She also came to know Christ at a young age.

Ramzi and Layla got along well and developed a very deep friendship. They were not only study mates but had deep fellowship together. After they graduated from medical school they got married, opened two practices in the same office in a middle-class area of Cairo, and rented an apartment near their office.

Since they both graduated from lower-class areas of Cairo, they decided to leave the two churches they knew and join another Protestant church in the same area where they lived and worked. On their first Sunday, as they arrived at the church, there was an older man who happened to be an elder standing at the door greeting people. When he met them, he was a bit too inquisitive, asking them where they lived and where they were from. Ramzi did not like him, but finally the elder got busy meeting other people and Ramzi and his wife were able to go into the church. They liked the service and decided this would be their future church. The only negative that Ramzi and Layla could think of was the elder at the door greeting people. *Will he be there next Sunday?* they wondered.

The following Sunday, as they parked their car and walked to the church door, that same elder was there greeting people. When he saw them and remembered them, he broke into a big smile and wanted to know more about them. So again he asked them where they came from. Ramzi sternly gave him his home and office address, pointing out clearly that they lived in a middle-class area. The elder apologized for not making his question clear. He wanted to know where Ramzi and Layla grew up. Where did their parents live? Perhaps he could tell from their accents that they weren't originally from the area.

Ramzi and Layla were embarrassed about their lower-class upbringing. They wanted to detach themselves from their past. Does Paul have anything to say to Ramzi and Layla in 1 Corinthians 7:21-24? He says to them,

> There is nothing wrong with upward mobility. If you can move to the middle class that is fine, but do not do it for the wrong reasons. Actually, there would have been nothing wrong in having opened your office in a lower-class area of Cairo. You could have lived as well in that area and might have ended up as the most educated people in that part of the city. Ramzi and Layla, as you embrace your heritage and your family backgrounds, *do not focus on your upward mobility; focus instead on the mobility and the expansion of the gospel* through your lives.

As we have seen, this chapter in 1 Corinthians is a chapter on family life. Yet in the middle of the chapter, in verses 17-24, there is a nugget of truth. This nugget could have been placed as well in other letters of Paul. The nugget addressed a marriage and family issue but also the Jew/Gentile controversy and the slavery issue.

Some Muslims, upon putting their faith in Christ, want to leave Islam completely and get integrated into Christianity. Others, if they are given the option, would prefer to remain in their contexts and work on cleaning the channels of relationships. As Christians, *we should provide both options to the Muslims* with whom we are sharing the gospel. These Muslim seekers could be easily *steered* or *manipulated* to favor our cultural or theological biases. They *deserve better.*

## QUESTIONS FOR REFLECTION AND DISCUSSION

1. Go back to the beginning of the chapter. What do you think of the strong statement that the Syrian Christian made: "Can you imagine a Satan worshiper staying in his Satan worshipers' church in order to be salt and light among his own people? Islam is evil, and no one can stay within Islam as an insider." Do you think that a Muslim who believes in Christ can remain in his Muslim context with his relationships intact?

2. Can you think of other texts in the Scriptures that allow, or even encourage, the remaining-in-context approach to ministry with Muslims? What do you like about these texts?

3. What stood out to you from the story of Naaman in 2 Kings 5?

4. What theological legitimacy is presented in 1 Corinthians 7:17-24 for the remaining-in-context approach? What strong arguments do you find? In what way does this passage adequately address and face squarely this approach?

# CHAPTER 17

# WHERE TO GO FROM HERE

We Christians in the West (and other Christians around the world influenced by the West) tend to look at reality with a set of lenses colored by the Bible, by our church doctrines, and by our distinct culture. It is as if we constantly wear tinted lenses — let's say brown sunglasses — and we tend to assume that what we see is the real color. In contrast, Muslims tend to wear a different set of tinted glasses — perhaps green sunglasses. Because of their religious background, they tend to see the world in a distinct manner that is different from ours. They assume as well that what they see through their green lenses is the real and only color. In this book, we have had the opportunity to look at our world through the eyes — through the green sunglasses — of Ahmad as a composite and through the eyes of his dad and sister through their contributions. My hope is that seeing the world through their eyes has helped us realize that we, too, wear sunglasses, although they are different from the Muslims'. Coming to the realization that we have a worldview colored by our culture is a great step on the way to becoming cross-cultural.

In this book I tried to unpack and address the issues raised by Ahmad under the two categories "Your Message" and "Me, the Receiver." The issues that he raised about us in the category "You, the Messenger" are outside the scope of this book, although they are very important issues. Christians in the West carry baggage that other Christians in the world do not carry. The additional chapters found in the separate addendum address our Western baggage and other issues associated with the history of Christendom and our perceptions of current events. Those of you who, *after reading this book, want to go deeper can contact me* at nabeel@nabeeljabbour.com, and I will send you the chapters that deal with the Crusades, colonialism, the history of Israel, and eschatology. I would be glad to send you those chapters as an e-mail attachment. The *condition*, though, is *having read the book.*

## Learning from the Book of Jonah

Years ago I used to assume that the book of Jonah was a typical missionary story. The missionary leaves his country and goes to a very distant land—the farther away the more glorious—and proclaims the Bible's message. As a result, a huge breakthrough takes place and many Gentiles turn to God in repentance. I used to assume that the main focus of the book of Jonah was the conversion of thousands upon thousands of pagans in the city of Nineveh. But soon I came to realize that the book of Jonah is not primarily the story of the conversion of the Ninevites. Rather it is primarily the story of a servant of God who needed to be converted. After the conversion of the Ninevites, one would expect that Jonah would rejoice as God lavished His grace on the Gentiles and forgave them when they demonstrated true repentance. Instead we see Jonah greatly displeased and very angry. His prayer reveals his rotten attitude and the great need he had to be *converted*—to repent and to have a heart like the heart of God toward the Gentiles. In his prayer he demonstrated clearly his ethnocentricity and his prejudice against the Gentiles. He said, "O Lord, is this not what I said when I was still at home? That is why I was so quick to flee to Tarshish. I knew that you are a gracious and compassionate God, slow to anger and abounding in love. . . . Take away my life" (4:2-3). What was he saying? I will paraphrase it and perhaps exaggerate a little bit for shock purposes and to make a point. I think Jonah was saying to God,

> Lord, you know my heart — my commitment and my zeal to go to the Gentiles with a message of judgment. But I do not trust you because at times you tend to become mushy and compassionate. If I could trust you I would have obeyed you from the beginning when you wanted me to go to Nineveh. That is the reason I did not obey you and headed instead in the opposite direction to Tarshish. But you brought me here by force and here we are and you are proving my point. I would rather die.

David Bosch commented on the book of Jonah by saying, "The story's missionary significance does not lie in the physical journey of a prophet of God to a pagan country, but in Yahweh being a God of compassion — a compassion which has no boundaries."[1]

When you read chapters 2, 3, and 4, with the input of Ahmad, his dad, and his sister, Fatima, what thoughts did you have? Were you wrestling with Ahmad and his family in your mind? For my part, after Ahmad's last visit to our home when he read to me what he had written about the Muslim worldview, I went to bed and could not sleep. Some of these questions were very much on my mind:

1. Who is my neighbor? Muslims are 1.4 billion people, more than 20 percent of the world's population.

2. What is true in what Ahmad is saying?

3. Is there something I need to confess to God and ask forgiveness for from this man on behalf of my fellow citizens and fellow Christians? Nehemiah asked God to forgive him and the Jews in Jerusalem although he was living in Babylon and did not sin against God as his people did in Jerusalem.

4. In what areas do I need to learn more concerning the issues that Ahmad raised? What are the resources? Could the additional chapters on the Crusades, colonialism, the history of Israel, and eschatology be helpful to me?

5. In some of what Ahmad is saying, is there a misconception on his part or on my part? How can I know?

6. Which of the issues that Ahmad raised deal with our Western "wrappings" around the gospel, and which deal with the essence of the gospel?

7. How can I learn to make the gospel available in ways other than my familiar paradigm?

8. What are the proper comparisons between Islam and Christianity?

9. What sources of apologetics are available to me?

10. How can I communicate in humility and compassion without having to agree with Ahmad on everything?

11. Which of my conclusions and assumptions on the modern history of the Middle East should I revisit?

12. How would I describe my attitude toward the undecided one billion Muslims on earth? What can I do to attract them — one person at a time — through Chistlikeness to become more open-minded and moderate?

13. How can Muslims remain within their Muslim culture as true and committed followers of Christ?

14. Does God want me to commit myself to praying for the Muslim world on a regular basis starting with a Muslim I know?

# ADDENDUM

The chapters in my addendum have to do with us, the messengers. I did not want to include this in the bulk of the book, partly because most of it is not material that is original with me. The other reason is that these chapters could discourage some readers from reading a thick book. These additional chapters are for those readers who want to understand why Muslims perceive us in a way very different from how we perceive ourselves. Hopefully, many of those who read this book to the end will desire to read the addendum chapters as well and will get motivated to go more in depth in their reading and study so that they will have a better understanding of how Muslims think and how they see the world. Becoming cross-cultural implies a desire on our part to cross over to their world. Christ did not declare His message to us from heaven. He came down to earth and lived in our broken world. He crossed over to our culture and experienced the limitations of time and space. He knew what it is to feel emotional pain, sorrow, hunger, and physical suffering. Just before His ascension into heaven He told His disciples, "As the Father has sent me, I am sending you" (John 20:21).

Another reason for not including the addendum in the book is that I want to continue to update it. Since one of the objectives of the addendum is to encourage the reader to get deeper into the issues by reading helpful books, there will always be new books that are worth reading. So the addendum will be updated as necessary.

The addendum will unpack and address the issues that Ahmad raised under the category "You, the Western Christian Messenger." Those chapters will address the Crusades, Colonialism, Modern History of Israel, and Eschatology. The addendum will also include some appendices of helpful articles addressing current events.

A very good friend of mine who is serving the Lord among Muslims in a third world country helped me review this manuscript before its publication. After sending him the addendum, he sent me this message:

> I am through with the chapters in the addendum. But those chapters trouble me. I was shocked reading the chapters on the Crusades, neocolonialism, and Zionism. Even in my sleep last night I felt haunted.

After reading his message, I did not understand what he meant. Was I wrong in writing these chapters for the addendum? Should I get rid of them? So I asked him to explain more. He wrote back,

> This is a great book with a very important addendum! It was these ugly layers that shocked me. *The book and the addendum are right on course!* I had not realized how much the gospel has been calcified in layers of violent history and rhetoric. I searched for and found that sermon by Urban II. I have read it and other history books before but have been blind to how the Muslims see and feel about us. I called one of my Muslim

friends yesterday and asked him to forgive me. This, I hope in a small way in a little corner here, will help bring a community of humility toward each other. My history is as guilty of terrorism as theirs. The situation at the moment is the kettle calling the pot black. Perhaps, though it is not a justification, my history made it easy for them to be angry.

In other words, these chapters in the addendum are such well-written and thought-provoking chapters that they hit me like a thunderbolt. I feel I stand on level ground with the Muslims when it comes to prejudice and violence. My history is not holier than theirs. I should therefore increase my tolerance level and point them to Jesus, not Christianity. This book and its addendum are thus right on target. I am the first beneficiary!

When I told my Muslim friend two days ago that I was not asking him to become a Christian but only to believe in Christ, he said, "You are just changing strategy." He brought up the issue of the Crusades. He didn't believe me. I have known him for ten years. But I sowed the wrong DNA many years back. That is why I felt haunted. That is why I called him back the next day and apologized again.

Again, the addendum is available by e-mail attachment if you wish to write me at nabeel@nabeeljabbour.com. Please send me your request with the title: Addendum.

# ENDNOTES

## PREFACE

1. Brennan Manning, *Abba's Child: The Cry of the Heart for Intimate Belonging* (Colorado Springs, CO: NavPress, 2002), 68–69. Original source: Stephen Covey, *The Seven Habits of Highly Effective People*, audiocassette seminar (Provo, UT).

## CHAPTER 1: WHY BOTHER?

1. Nabeel Jabbour, *The Rumbling Volcano: Islamic Fundamentalism in Egypt* (Pasadena, CA: Mandate Press, 1993), 8.
2. Edward Said, *Orientalism* (New York: Vintage Books, 1979), 67.
3. Samuel Huntington, *The Clash of Civilizations and the Remaking of World Order* (New York: Simon & Schuster, Touchtone, 1996).

## CHAPTER 2: AHMAD'S WORLDVIEW

1. UN Office for the Coordination of Humanitarian Affairs, "Iraq: Child Mortality Rates Finally Dropping," *IRIN:*

*Humanitarian News and Analysis*, http://www.irinnews.org/report.
aspx?reportid=25417 (accessed July 3, 2007).

## CHAPTER 3: THEIR GRIEVANCES

1. Jimmy Carter, *Our Endangered Values* (New York: Simon &
   Schuster Paperbacks, 2005), 1.
2. John Ortberg, *If You Want to Walk on Water, You've Got to Get out
   of the Boat* (Grand Rapids, MI: Zondervan), 2001.
3. David Bosch, *Transforming Mission* (Maryknoll, NY: Orbis Books,
   1991).
4. For example, see Rashid Khalidi's *The Iron Cage: The Story of the
   Palestinian's Struggle for Statehood* (Boston: Beacon Press, 2006).

## CHAPTER 4: AHMAD'S SISTER

1. In this section, I am indebted to Shirin Taber, *Muslims Next Door:
   Uncovering Myths and Creating Friendships* (Grand Rapids, MI:
   Zondervan, 2004).
2. In this section, I am indebted to Benazir Bhutto, "Politics and the
   Muslim Woman," in *Liberal Islam*, ed. Charles Kurzman (Oxford:
   Oxford University Press, 1998), 107–111.

## CHAPTER 5: THE DRIVING FORCE OF ASSUMPTIONS

1. Rick Warren, *The Purpose Driven Life* (Grand Rapids, MI:
   Zondervan, 2002), 49.
2. John Clark Mead, *The New World War* (Fairfax, VA: Xulon Press,
   2002), 47.
3. Nabeel Jabbour, *The Rumbling Volcano: Islamic Fundamentalism in
   Egypt* (Pasadena, CA: Mandate Press, 1993), 125.

## CHAPTER 6: THE CORE AND THE WRAPPINGS

1. The first half of my earlier book, *Unshackled and Growing*, deals with Christ being the good news. *Unshackled and Growing* (Colorado Springs, CO: Dawson Media, 2006).
2. This list and the tangerine illustration come from my book *Unshackled and Growing*, chapter 1.

## CHAPTER 7: MILITANCY OR TOLERANCE

1. Darryl Fears and Claudia Deanne, "Negative Perception of Islam Increasing." *Washington Post*, March 9, 2006, A01.
2. Quoted in Charles Kurzman, ed., *Liberal Islam: A Sourcebook* (Oxford: Oxford University Press, 1998), 234.

## CHAPTER 10: THE POWER OF PARADIGMS

1. Roland Muller, *Honor and Shame: Unlocking the Door* (Philadelphia: Xlibris Corporation, 2001). www.rmuller.com.
2. For more information about Dr. Bailey and his books, see his website, www.shenango.org/bailey.htm.

## CHAPTER 11: SHAME, DEFILEMENT, AND FEAR

1. See Waldron Scott's website, http://www.waldronscott.net.
2. Bruce McCluggage, "Bartolome de las Casas, From Conquest to Advocacy" (lecture, Rocky Mountain Region of the Evangelical Missiological Society, Denver, CO, April 21, 2006).

## CHAPTER 13: THE BIBLE AND THE QUR'AN

1. John Gilchrist, *The Qur'an: The Scripture of Islam* (South Africa: MERCSA, 1995). Other books by Gilchrist include *Muhammad: The Prophet of Islam* and *Facing the Muslim Challenge*. All are available on the Internet at http://answering-islam.org. uk/Gilchrist/#qbs.

CHAPTER 15: DIVERSITY OF MANIFESTATIONS

1. Nabeel Jabbour, *Unshackled and Growing: Muslims and Christians on the Journey to Freedom* (Colorado Springs, CO: Dawson Media, 2006), chapter 11.

CHAPTER 17: WHERE TO GO FROM HERE

1. David Bosch, *Witness to the World* (Atlanta: John Knox, 1980), 53.

# WORKS CITED

Abdullahi Ahmed An-Na'im. *Shari'a and Basic Human Rights Concerns*. Oxford: Oxford University Press, 1998.

Gilchrist, John. *The Qur'an: The Scripture of Islam*. South Africa: MERSCA, 1995. Available free at http://answering-islam.org.uk/Gilchrist/#qbs.

Kurzman, Charles, ed. *Liberal Islam: A Sourcebook*. Oxford: Oxford University Press, 1998.

Manning, Brennan. *Abba's Child: The Cry of the Heart for Intimate Belonging*. Colorado Springs, CO: NavPress, 2002.

Mead, John Clark. *The New World War*. Longwood, FL: Xulon Press, 2002.

Muller, Roland. *Honor and Shame: Unlocking the Door*. Philadelphia: Xlibris Corporation, 2001. Available free at www.rmuller.com.

Scott, Waldron. Website at http://www.waldronscott.net.

Taber, Shirin. *Muslims Next Door: Uncovering Myths and Creating Friendships*. Grand Rapids, MI: Zondervan, 2004.

Warren, Rick. *The Purpose Driven Life*. Grand Rapids, MI: Zondervan, 2002.

## ADDITIONAL RECOMMENDED READING LIST

*30 Days Muslim Prayer Focus*. Colorado Springs, CO: World Christian News & Books. To order copies, contact 719-380-0507 or http://www.30daysprayer.com/muslim/. To sign up for the e-mail version, which will automatically be sent to your e-mail address each day, send an e-mail to 30-days-on@ls.pmbx.net.

Carter, Jimmy. *Palestine: Peace Not Apartheid*. New York: Simon & Schuster, 2006.

Chacour, Elias. *Blood Brothers*. Grand Rapids, MI: Chosen Books, 2003.

Chapman, Colin. *Cross and Crescent: Responding to the Challenge of Islam*. Downers Grove, IL: InterVarsity, 2003.

*The Holy Injil: First Book — Matthew*. Colorado Springs, CO: International Bible Society. This is the gospel of Matthew in user-friendly English language for Muslims. It refers to God as Allah and to Jesus as Isa. To get a copy, write to P.O. Box 35700, Colorado Springs, CO, 80935-3570 or call 719-488-9200.

Hoskins, Edward J. *A Muslim's Heart: What Every Christian Needs to Know to Share Christ with Muslims*. Colorado Springs, CO: Dawson Media, 2003.

Jabbour, Nabeel. *The Rumbling Volcano: Islamic Fundamentalism in Egypt*. Pasadena, CA: Mandate Press, 1993.

Jabbour, Nabeel. *The Unseen Reality: A Panoramic View of Spiritual Warfare*. Available free at www.nabeeljabbour.com.

Jabbour, Nabeel. *Unshackled and Growing: Muslims and Christians on the Journey to Freedom.* Colorado Springs, CO: Dawson Media, 2006.

Jabbour, Nabeel. Website at www.nabeeljabbour.com. Links to more than one hundred websites under various categories.

Janssen, Al and Brother Andrew. *Light Force: A Stirring Account of the Church Caught in the Middle East Crossfire.* Grand Rapids, MI: Revell, 2004.

Johnstone, Patrick. *Operation World.* Grand Rapids, MI: Zondervan, 2001.

Piper, John. "Israel, Palestine, and the Middle East." Sermon, March 7, 2004, http://www.desiringgod.org/ResourceLibrary/Sermons/ByDate/2004/165_Israel_Palestine_and_the_Middle_East/.

# ABOUT THE AUTHOR

DR. NABEEL T. JABBOUR was born in Syria and grew up in Lebanon. He lived with his family in Egypt for fifteen years before moving to Colorado Springs, his current home where he works with The Navigators. With a doctorate in Islamics, Dr. Jabbour is a professor and frequent lecturer at seminaries and churches around the world. He is also the author of *Unshackled and Growing*, *The Rumbling Volcano*, and *The Unseen Reality*. For more information, go to www.nabeeljabbour.com.

# Check out these other great titles from NavPress!

## Building Bridges
Fouad Elias Accad
ISBN-13: 978-0-89109-795-2

This book supplies readers with the information, concrete examples, and insights necessary when dialoguing with Muslims. If you want to reach out to Muslims around you, *Building Bridges* will equip you to build relationships of mutual respect and trust.

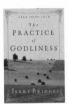

## The Practice of Godliness
Jerry Bridges
ISBN-13: 978-0-89109-941-3

In *The Practice of Godliness*, Jerry Bridges examines what it means to grow in Christian character and helps us establish the foundation upon which that character is built. Bridges opens our eyes to see how character formation affects the way we relate to God, ourselves, and others.

To order copies, call NavPress at 1-800-366-7788 or log on to www.navpress.com.

NAVPRESS

Discipleship Inside Out™

# More titles from NavPress!

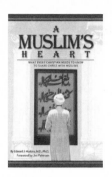

## A Muslim's Heart

Dr. Edward J. Hoskins
ISBN: 978-0-96724-806-6

In an age when Christians are often more fearful and suspicious of Muslims than warm and relational, *A Muslim's Heart* will help you understand Muslim culture and how to share Christ within that context. A practical, quick-to-read guide, this book is ideal for those befriending Muslims overseas and in their own U.S. neighborhoods.

## Unshackled & Growing: Muslims and Christians on the Journey to Freedom

Nabeel T. Jabbour
ISBN: 978-0-97290-232-8

Do you know Muslims who are put off by Christianity yet are intrigued by Christ? *Unshackled & Growing* is written just for them, answering their questions about Jesus in culturally-sensitive ways and helping them walk with God and grow in discipleship in an atmosphere of grace. Although the primary audience for this book is English-speaking Muslims, Muslim-background believers and even Christians will be challenged by the book's message to move beyond a life of legalism and experience the grace and truth offered by Christ.

To order copies, call NavPress at 1-800-366-7788 or
log on to www.navpress.com.

NAVPRESS

Discipleship Inside Out™